# Prepare for the Great Tribulation and the Era of Peace

# Prepare for the Great Tribulation and the Era of Peace

## Volume XII:
## July 1, 1998 – September 30, 1998

by John Leary

**PUBLISHING COMPANY**
P.O. Box 42028 Santa Barbara, CA 93140-2028
(800) 647-9882 • (805) 957-4893 • Fax: (805) 957-1631

The publisher recognizes and accepts that the final authority regarding these apparitions and messages rests with the Holy See of Rome, to whose judgement we willingly submit.

– The Publisher

Cover art by Josyp Terelya

©1998 Queenship Publishing - All Rights Reserved

Library of Congress Number # 95-73237

Published by:
    Queenship Publishing
    P.O. Box 42028
    Santa Barbara, CA 93140-2028
    (800) 647-9882 • (805) 957-4893 • Fax: (805) 957-1631

Printed in the United States of America

ISBN: 1-57918-105-8

# Acknowledgments

It is in a spirit of deep gratitude that I would like to acknowledge first the Holy Trinity: Father, Jesus, and the Holy Spirit, the Blessed Virgin Mary and the many saints and angels who have made this book possible.

My wife, Carol, has been an invaluable partner. Her complete support of faith and prayers has allowed us to work as a team. This was especially true in the many hours of indexing and proofing of the manuscript. All of our family has been a source of care and support.

I am greatly indebted to Josyp Terelya for his very gracious offer to provide the art work for this publication. He has spent three months of work and prayer to provide us with a selection of many original pictures. He wanted very much to enhance the visions and messages with these beautiful and provocative works. You will experience some of them throughout these volumes.

A very special thank you goes to my spiritual director, Fr. Leo J. Klem, C.S.B. No matter what hour I called him, he was always there with his confident wisdom, guidance and discernment. His love, humility, deep faith and trust are a true inspiration.

My appreciation also goes to Father John V. Rosse, my good pastor who is retiring from Holy Name of Jesus Church. He has been open, loving and supportive from the very beginning.

There are many friends and relatives whose interest, love and prayerful support have been a real gift from God. Our own Wednesday, Monday and First Saturday prayer groups deserve a special thank you for their loyalty and faithfulness.

Finally, I would like to thank Bob and Claire Schaefer of Queenship Publishing for providing the opportunity to bring this message of preparation, love and warnings to you the people of God.

John Leary, Jr.

# Dedication

To the Most Holy Trinity

God

The Father, Son and Holy Spirit

The Source of

All

Life, Love and Wisdom

# Publisher's Foreword

John has, with some exceptions, been having visions twice a day since they began in July, 1993. The first vision of the day usually takes place during morning Mass, immediately after he receives the Eucharist. If the name of the church is not mentioned, it is a local Rochester, NY, church. When out of town, the church name is included in the text. The second vision occurs in the evening, either at Perpetual Adoration or at the prayer group that is held at Holy Name of Jesus Church.

Various names appear in the text. Most of the time, the names appear only once or twice. Their identity is not important to the message and their reason for being in the text is evident. First names have been used, when requested by the individual.

We are grateful to Josyp Terelya for the cover art, as well as for the art throughout the book. Josyp is a well-known visionary and also, the author of *Witness* and most recently *In the Kingdom of the Spirit.*

This volume covers messages from July 1, 1998 through September 30, 1998. The volumes have been coming out quarterly due to the urgency of the messages.

Volume I: July, 1993 through June, 1994.
Volume II: July, 1994 through June, 1995.
Volume III: July, 1995 through July 10, 1996.
Volume IV: July 11, 1996 through September 30, 1996.
Volume V: October 1, 1996 through December 31, 1996.
Volume VI: January 1, 1997 through March 31, 1997.
Volume VII: April 1, 1997 through June 30, 1997.
Volume VIII: July 1, 1997 through September 30, 1997.
Volume IX: October 1, 1997 through December 31, 1997.
Volume X: January 1, 1998 through March 31, 1998.
Volume XI: April 1, 1998 through June 30, 1998.

The Publisher

# Foreword

It was in July of 1993 that Almighty God, especially through Jesus, His Eternal Word, entered the life of John Leary in a most remarkable way. John is 56 years old and is a retired chemist from Eastman Kodak Co., Rochester, New York. He lives in a modest house in the suburbs of Rochester with Carol, his wife of thirty-three years, and Catherine, his youngest daughter. His other two daughters, Jeanette and Donna, are married and have homes of their own. John has been going to daily Mass since he was seventeen and has been conducting a weekly prayer group in his own home for twenty-five years. For a long time, he has been saying fifteen decades of the Rosary each day.

In April of 1993 he and his wife made a pilgrimage to Our Lady's shrine in Medjugorje, Yugoslavia. While there, he felt a special attraction to Jesus in the Blessed Sacrament. There he became aware that the Lord Jesus was asking him to change his way of life and to make Him his first priority. A month later in his home, Our Lord spoke to him and asked if he would give over his will to Him to bring about a very special mission. Without knowing clearly to what he was consenting, John, strong in faith and trust, agreed to all the Lord would ask.

On July 21, 1993 the Lord gave him an inkling of what would be involved in this new calling. He was returning home from Toronto in Canada where he had listened to a talk of Maria Esperanza (a visionary from Betania, Venezuela) and had visited Josyp Terelya. While in bed, he had a mysterious interior vision of a newspaper headline that spelled "DISASTER." Thus began a series of daily and often twice daily interior visions along with messages, mostly from Jesus. Other messages were from God the Father, the Holy Spirit, the Blessed Virgin Mary, his guardian angel and many of the saints, especially St. Therese of Lisieux. These messages he recorded on his word processor. In the beginning, they were quite short, but they became more extensive as the weeks passed by. At the time of this writing, he is still receiving visions and messages.

These daily spiritual experiences, which occur most often immediately following Communion, consist of a brief vision which becomes the basis of the message that follows. They range widely on a great variety of subjects, but one might group them under the following categories: warnings, teachings and love messages. Occasionally, there are personal confirmations of some special requests that he made to the Lord.

The interior visions contain an amazing number of different pictures, some quite startling, which hardly repeat themselves. In regard to the explicit messages that are inspired by each vision, they contain deep insights into the kind of relationship God wishes to establish with His human creatures. There, also, is an awareness of how much He loves us and yearns for our response. As a great saint once wrote: "Love is repaid only by love." On the other hand, God is not a fool to be treated lightly. In fact, did not Jesus once say something about not casting pearls before the swine? Thus, there are certain warnings addressed to those who shrug God off as if He did not exist or is not important in human life.

Along with such warnings, we become more conscious of the reality of Satan and the forces of evil "...which wander through the world seeking the ruin of souls." We used to recite this at the end of each low Mass. In His love and concern for us, Our Lord keeps constantly pointing out how frail we humans are in the face of such evil angelic powers. God is speaking of the necessity of daily prayer, of personal penance, and of turning away from atheistic and material enticements which are so much a part of our modern environment.

Perhaps the most controversial parts of the messages are those which deal with what we commonly call Apocalyptic. Unusual as these may be, in my judgment, they are not basically any different than what we find in the last book of the New Testament or in some of the writings of St. Paul. After a careful and prayerful reading of the hundreds of pages in this book, I have not found anything contrary to the authentic teaching authority of the Roman

Catholic Church.

The 16th Century Spanish mystic, St. John of the Cross, gives us sound guidelines for discerning the authenticity of this sort of phenomena involving visions, locutions, etc. According to him, there are three possible sources: the devil, some kind of self-imposed hypnosis or God. I have been John's spiritual confidant for over five years. I have tested him in various spiritual ways and I am most confident that all he has put into these messages is neither of the devil nor of some kind of mental illness. Rather, they are from the God who, in His love for us, wishes to reveal His own Divine mind and heart. He has used John for this. I know that John is quite ready to abide by any decision of proper ecclesiastical authority on what he has written in this book.

Rev. Leo J. Klem, C.S.B.
Rochester, New York
1993

# Visions and Messages of John Leary:

**Wednesday, July 1, 1998:**
   After Communion, I could see a small window that had been broken. Jesus said: **"My people, the sins of the flesh committed in privacy are still serious sins according to the teachings of my Church and My Commandments. No matter whether people think they are not serious or even if priests say they are not sins, I still judge these offenses to be mortal sins. These are fornication, adultery, masturbation, sex before marriage, and unnatural birth control. My pope son has spoken out against many of these sins as serious. Some sinners are still in denial that these are sins or serious sin. They do not want to be deprived of their right to sinful pleasures. Your priests should be preaching of the dangers of these sins, and if they deny they are sins or serious sins, then do not believe them and go to a holy priest for Confession. In your heart you know these are sins against the marriage act as I have intended it to be. So refrain from these sins and seek My forgiveness in Confession. Whenever you commit such sins, get to Confession as soon as possible. There are more souls going to Hell for these unconfessed sins than any other sins."**

**Thursday, July 2, 1998:**
   After Communion, I could see a whip as someone was about to be flogged. Jesus said: **"My people, I was persecuted and scourged for claiming that I was the Son of God before the high priest. You too will be asked to publicly proclaim your belief in Me. Evil men who detest you for your beliefs will try to whip you into submission, but their attempts will be futile. My prophets have been tortured and killed down through the**

ages, because the rulers and the people did not want to listen to their judgments. These rulers wanted to continue in their sins of pleasure, but the prophecies did come true and many rulers were brought to their own ruin that they deserved. My judgments are true and those things foretold by My prophets were warnings. When those warned refused to change their sinful lives, My wrath was carried out on them or their children. So, listen to My prophets and heed their warnings before it is too late and you are condemned in your sins."

Later, at the prayer group, I could see water being poured out of a gold pail from Heaven. Jesus said: "My people, I have shown you before that some of your areas will receive too much rain and have floods, while other areas will receive little causing droughts and fires. You are being tested dearly because it is the only way to get your attention and bring you to your knees. You are being stripped of your possessions as one event will fall after another. Pray that sinners will change their lives and then these things would be mitigated."

I could see a house in a flood with only the open windows to see through two holes. Jesus said: "My people, you have witnessed many severe thunderstorms in a short time and these will continue to saturate certain areas. Flooding and fires have occurred before, but they are now increasing in intensity as few are repenting of their sins. When your country seeks My forgiveness of your sins, only then will your troubles subside. Your One World people will take advantage of your shortages and they will try to prepare you to follow the Antichrist. Seek My help and you will spiritually survive this evil age."

I could see a waste container for trash. Jesus said: "My people, since you have made material things your idols, I will destroy them before you to show you how quickly they fade. Those things that you have grown to depend on will be taken away and then you will have to seek My help to answer all of your needs. Place your trust in Me who lasts forever and not material things which will be thrown into the fire tomorrow. Many are seeing their homes, cars, and furniture being destroyed by floods and fires. Get on your knees, America, and I will listen to your pleadings for My help."

I could see many saints dressed in white robes with a bright light coming from them. Jesus said: "**My people, strive every day to live in My Divine Will, always following My Plan for you. You all have the ability to be saints, so reach out to imitate the saints in your prayers and in your actions. Continue to focus on a good spiritual life and help Me in bringing souls to Me. The more times you reach out to sinners in My Name, the more chances you have to save souls. Encourage souls to come to Confession and have good prayer lives.**"

I could see some old vintage cars. Jesus said: "**My people, your cars will become scarce and hard to find and afford. With all of the difficulties going on, it will be harder to fuel your car and keep it from damage. As your driving becomes more impaired, you will see your usual comforts will be threatened. Be grateful for what little you have and do not seek these things out of greed and pride. You will see in the end that only spiritual things have any lasting value.**"

I could see some calm fluffy clouds being bathed in sunlight. Jesus said: "**My people, look forward in hope and trust that one day these clouds of evil filth will be removed from the earth. I will bring about the defeat of the evil ones in My time. Be patient but a moment and you will soon share in My Era of Peace. The joy that you will share in My New Jerusalem will be worth suffering this short tribulation. So, prepare for this trial which will truly test your love for Me.**"

I could see a modern store that was giving people the option to get their Mark of the Beast. Jesus said: "**My people, the evil men are preparing your new means for buying and selling both on the computer and in fancy new stores using the chips. You will have smart cards offered to you as a choice at first. Later, these smart cards will be forced on you to buy and sell as the only means possible for transactions. Then they will try and force you to take these chips in the hand or forehead or you will not be able to buy and sell. Many will be imprisoned, tortured, martyred and enslaved for refusing to take the Mark of the Beast. Be ready, My faithful, to flee into hiding with your guardian angels. With trust in My help, all of your needs will be provided for. Do not worship the Antichrist or take any help from him as the chip in the hand.**"

**Friday, July 3, 1998:** (St. Thomas the Apostle)

After Communion, I could see a host being raised at a Mass and behind it was an adobe building with wood rafters protruding. Jesus said: **"My people, just as My Apostles went out to many nations to spread My Gospel, all of My faithful are called as well to witness My Resurrection.** My Word has been taken to many nations, but still many do not want to believe. Even St. Thomas doubted in the reality of My Resurrection, but once he was shown My wounds, he believed with an inspiring faith. Many people need physical proof to believe things, but blessed are they who believe without this evidence. All humanity has this proof of My Resurrection in the negative image of My shroud in Turin. Even those viewing such evidence still do not want to believe in Me. Now you know that faith in Me is truly a blessed gift. It is not an acceptance by earthly understanding, but those, who believe, have been touched by My grace and have accepted Me on faith alone. It is not easy to understand God becoming a man, but believe in My Coming for man's salvation, since it is only through Me that you can be saved."

Later, at Holy Name I could see the earth out in space and many angels were descending on the earth. Jesus said: **"My people, My angels of protection are coming. They are marking My faithful with crosses on their foreheads. They will be your angels of protection at the places of refuge. They are the same angels that will cast the evil spirits and evil men into Hell where they will be chained. These spiritual beings are beautiful in appearance, yet they are powerful in their duty. It is by My Will that they will protect you from evil men and the demons. Give praise and glory to Me for all that I have planned for mankind. You will struggle for a while during the Tribulation, but through My help and My angels, they will provide for all of your needs."**

**Saturday, July 4, 1998:** (Independence Day)

After Communion, I could see our flag burning. Jesus said: **"My people, other countries are burning your flag, while you have to pass laws for your own people not to burn your flag. Those who refuse to fight for their freedoms will lose what little you have. Your President and Congress are in concert with the**

One World people to do away with all of your rights and freedoms. Your presidents have written enough executive orders to declare fiat tyranny at the start of martial law. You will be fortunate to have another presidential election. Many of your documents of independence declare My Name, but today My Name is banned by your distorted view of Church and state. The atheists have taken over your country and you do not even realize it. Your religious and other freedoms will slowly disappear before your eyes, because you have turned your back on Me. When you fail to give thanks to Me for all that you have, I will take away your blessings and watch you fall in ruin. How many times do I have to say to you, wake up America, or your days are numbered. Until you place Me back in your lives and stop your sins of pleasure and idol worship, your troubles with My chastisements will continue."

Later, at Adoration, I could see some fires starting and a massive flame came toward me. Jesus said: "My people, take a lesson from all of the fires in Florida. It is no coincidence that large parts of Florida are burning. Many sins of greed, power and pleasure are going on there. This is a cleansing fire to strip people of their worship of materialism. Man thinks he can control things, but you see that My plan is being carried out first. No matter how much you think you can do on your own, you are better to trust in My help than your own devices. My ways are always better than your ways. So, follow My plan for your life, rather than any of your own selfish plans. You will see that My plan is always the best for your soul and requires less effort on your part. You try to force things to happen for your own benefit. I have you helping many souls to salvation, instead of you wasting your time on frivolous things of no meaning. So, continue to follow the prompting of My Spirit and you will be led down the road to Heaven."

### Sunday, July 5, 1998:

After Communion, I could see a flat horizon and then a huge wall of flame where the whole picture was orange red. Jesus said: "My people, I am showing you this inferno as a taste of Hell for those judged unworthy of Heaven. You have seen unusual fires of large proportion. This searing heat during the summer will continue to offer opportunities for fires. Again, if enough prayer comes forth, you can mitigate some of the damage. If you refuse to change your lives despite these signs, more fires will consume you. Man has been challenging My justice by the evil that he has committed. Without remorse for your sins, My punishment must fall, as it did on Israel. When your crops have withered and your comforts have been threatened, only then will you see dependence on Me is a necessity. Your riches and your defenses will be drawn away, and you will be ripe for the Antichrist's takeover. Pray now, for your spiritual strength will be tested."

Later, at Adoration, I could see a swollen river in a canyon. I then saw lightening and tornadoes coming from a very dark sky in daytime. Jesus said: "My people, your weather is not letting up with its fierce winds and rains. Many places, especially in the northern states, have seen strong, heavy rains cause some flooding. Many areas are experiencing higher than average rainfall, while other areas are drier than average. You have seen one event after another with no letup. All of these events are signs to you in the record heat and rainfalls. The news is constantly showing you the latest disasters. Still many have not made the connection between your unusual events and the increase in sin over the years. As more people turn their back on Me, I am making them more of an example in their disasters. Through lost possessions and electrical shortages, more families are coming in contact with My justice. How long will I rain destruction upon you to wake you up to following My Commands? I have waited and pleaded with you to change your ways, but these sufferings are the only way to get your attention. I call all of you out of love to follow My Will, but if man continues to insist on his sinful ways, he will reap the whirlwind of the consequences of sin. Come to Me in Confession to have your sins cleansed and forgiven. Without this sorrow for sin, how can you be saved? As you are brought low by hardships, you will be forced to seek My help. Even some areas are requesting rain in prayer. Keep these thoughts of conversion even after these trials, so you do not fall back into your old habits of serious sin."

**Monday, July 6, 1998:**

After Communion, I could see some birds and a white light came out of their midst. Jesus said: **"My people, I am showing you that miracles still happen among ordinary circumstances. You read in the Gospel of My curing of the woman with hemorrhages. The miracle of raising the girl from the dead may have overshadowed the previous miracle, but it still was a blessing. No matter how small or ordinary a miracle is, there is still a gift of faith present to make it happen. You have a miracle in your presence that you may consider ordinary. Every day at Mass there is a miracle when the priest consecrates the bread and wine into My Body and Blood. Again, without faith, this miracle would not be appreciated. By your recognizing My Real Presence in the Consecrated Host, you understand a miracle of far reaching importance among ordinary species. It is the presence of your God in the Host that truly makes My gift of the Eucharist so awesome. Rejoice and give thanks for all of My miracles, no matter how little."**

Later, I could see an old picture of a grandfather. Jesus said: **"My people, when you look on the walls and tables of your homes, many have pictures of their family members. You have these pictures because they represent a love bond between you. So it is with images and statues of Me, My mother Mary and the saints. You have these so you can remember the love between you and Me. I and the saints are with you in the comfort of your own homes. I love all of you as a part of My larger family of mankind. You all are capable of knowing Me and loving Me. I am a strong part of each of your families, for I unite all families through My love. When you look at pictures, they capture a moment in time of that person's life. When you view that person, they never change in appearance. This is very much like when you will live with Me in Heaven. When you exist in the eternal now, then you will be young forever. Just as you were captured in that moment of time, you will be sharing in My love and peace as you will be one with Me in your glorified bodies. Strive in your life to free yourself of your sins through My sacraments. By following My Will, even in your weakness, you will be on the road to the glory of your resurrec-**

Josyp Terelya

tion. When you are judged at the gates of Heaven, be prepared to make an accounting of your lives. By remembering Me in all that you do, you can focus on My image, so you can see My loving heart reaching out to you at all times."

**Tuesday, July 7, 1998:**

After Communion, I could see some rocky surfaces and a light shone against it. Jesus said: "**My people, I used the image of a rock when I called St. Peter to be the first pope of My Church. Of himself he could do nothing, but with the power of the Holy Spirit, he was inspired to spread the Gospel and even die for**

My sake. This light of faith is an image seen in the light against the rock. I enable each of My faithful to be firm in their faith and unyielding in their determination to do My Will. You have been blessed with many role models in the saints. Keep this image of stone present as you hold fast to your belief in Me and My Commands. I showed you before that the man who builds his house on rock will be able to weather the storms of life. When you have a firm foundation in faith through prayer and good works, then you too will be prepared to withstand the buffets of evil's temptations. Struggle every day to imitate this image of strength in the rock. Today, My Church is led by My Pope son, John Paul II. He is your rock of faith to follow in all of his decrees. Listen to him, because the Holy Spirit is working through him."

Later, at Adoration, I could see a large conference table with many important dignitaries around it. Jesus said: "My people, many secret arrangements are being made at these top level meetings. They are kept secret because the people would be upset if they saw their leaders selling out to the One World people. These evil men may control you for a while, but I will bring My victory over all of their plans. These men are struggling for power over the whole world. They are driven by Satan's desire to control the whole world for him through the Antichrist. You will see when one comes claiming to be Me, that his tyranny will be worse than some of your kings before him. The Antichrist will take advantage of his power to control food, jobs, and money. Do not be taken in by any of his lies or seeming miracles. Keep focused on doing My Will and refuse to cooperate with the Antichrist in taking his mark or taking any help from him. When you see how extensive his influence will be, you will want My help so you can be far from his clutches."

### Wednesday, July 8, 1998:

After Communion, I could see people at Church and a young girl was raised up. Jesus said: "My people, as I asked My Apostles to tend the lost sheep of Israel, you are seeing the children in your own families that need tending. Bring the children and your grandchildren up in the proper Faith as you have received.

By carrying on the Faith to your children, you are preserving the Faith to be carried on in succeeding generations. These are the new members of My Church that need guidance by good example in following My Will. The children learn their religion best from their parents. You parents are the role models that they look to in understanding your love for God. When they see you praying, going to Church, and going to Confession, this shows them that you believe in what you are preaching. Be careful not to give them bad example and show them the love that should be always a sign of your Christian faith. Once you have made an attempt to help your own household, now you are ready to evangelize those other souls around you. Seek My help and that of the Holy Spirit for the right words to speak in witnessing your faith to others."

**Thursday, July 9, 1998:**

After Communion, I could see a priest or an Apostle standing and then a close-up view of someone's eye looking around with a cave in the background. Jesus said: **"My people, today's Gospel speaks to all of My prophets and messengers. If you are truly spreading My message, it is not necessary to take money, but to rely on those helping you. Going to every opportunity, I have stressed as an important principle. There are so many souls that need conversion and so little time to accomplish this task. Many speak of a religious affiliation, but their hearts are far from Me. Even in America, your wealth and religious apathy have made your country a mission land, because they do not see a need for My help. Those whom I have called forth to evangelize I have given many graces and a strength in the Holy Spirit to go out and preach My Gospel. Those receiving My prophets should have their minds open and test the spirit of the truth being proclaimed. Those who listen and believe in My Words will be rewarded for helping My instruments, even if these chosen have some imperfections. You are always dealing with human weakness, so be open to forgive difficulties and iniquities. The main qualities that you should strive for are humility and truthfulness in My Word. Live in love of God and love of neighbor, always following My Will."**

Later, at the prayer group, I could see a chandelier with many lights and then an older woman watering her plants. Jesus said: **"My people, as you give the life giving water to your house plants, you also need to spiritually nourish those souls in need of My grace. Lead them to Me so they can be fed My sacraments. In the Eucharist of My Body and Blood you have the living water that will last forever. As persistent as you are to keep your plants from wilting, keep encouraging those in your family to stay close to Me. Pray and receive My sacraments often and My grace will be a fountain of strength for you."**

I could see some furniture covered over. Jesus said: **"My people, when you have a scratch or a hole in your furniture, you are quicker to cover it over than to repair it. So it is with your sins. You would rather try and forget them or cover them up with more lies than come to Confession. The evil one encourages you to be spiritually lazy and cover up rather than confess your sins. You have to make a forward decision and come to Me for the forgiveness of your sins. It is hard to put your pride down and admit that you are a sinner. But you must seek the priest in Confession to cleanse all of your sins and make you new in My grace."**

I could see an Asian picture with an orange light from the sun. Jesus said: **"My people, many nations in their greed for power and money, struggle in vain without My help. Many of these problems have fallen on the eastern countries because they were greedy for themselves instead of helping each other. You, America, have had bad times in the past and they will be returning. When you do not have God in your life, your life will be filled with disappointment because of your human failings. You may feel well now in your businesses, but be prepared when your good fortunes will be taken away from you. Have trust in My help and not in your money."**

I could see a bridge falling apart from a torrent of water pulling it one way and the other. Jesus said: **"My people, take heed of all of these events that are happening one right after the other. If there was any doubt that these are the End Times, more floods, fires and earthquakes are occurring more rapidly. Look in these signs and see that your earthly things are vulnerable** to destruction. Your spiritual treasures are protected forever, so seek these things in your spiritual acts of mercy. You run to gather valuable possessions, but why be frustrated by this fruitless endeavor. Seek only holy things and you will enjoy an eternal reward in Heaven."

I could see a very calm lake. Jesus said: "My people, you need to seek the calm waters of life instead of the excitement of the rapids. Man is always in search of adventure and risking his life for next to nothing but pride. Seek more to be humble in a quiet prayer life. When you are always on the run, it is hard to slow down to understand how life is passing you by. You are here to serve My Will and not just for your own pleasure. In prayer I can speak to your heart of what My Plan is for you. But unless you listen, how can you have time to open your heart to Me? Empty yourself of your will and replace it with My Will. Then I can mold you into the glorious soul you are meant to be."

I could see some gathering dark clouds of war. Jesus said: "My people, there are many regions in your world that are festering with hate. As you come upon harder times both financially and with the famine, these embers of hatred may be fanned into a major war. I have asked you many times to pray for peace in your world. Your weapons of war have become highly sophisticated and spread among many countries. Because you are in armed camps, it will take little to stir up some major trouble. Just one miscalculation could trigger a world war. Work on gaining peace through My love or you will indeed see the clouds of war overtake you."

I could see a door to a house and people were removing their shoes to enter. Jesus said: "My people, as you enter My House at church, you need to give My Blessed Sacrament proper respect. I am your God present in the Host of the Tabernacle. Give glory to Me by genuflecting and give Me honor by being quiet in front of Me and not with loud talking. My Presence is the reason that My Church is holy. You share in My Grace, but your holiness can be fleeting when your sins offend Me. When you come to visit Me, be more like the humble publican than the proud pharisee who has no need of My grace."

**Friday, July 10, 1998:**
After Communion, I could see some carnival structures over a Church. Jesus said: **"My people, when you come to Mass on Sunday, come in a prayerful mood and not just for a social gathering. When you enter your church, genuflect to My Real Presence in the Tabernacle. If your Tabernacle is in another room from the altar, stop to greet Me first, for I am the one who makes your church holy. It is important to give Me reverence and avoid a lot of loud talking in church. You come to Mass for only one hour for most, so make an effort to be at Mass on time. Also, do not be in a race to the parking lot. Give enough time to share those intimate moments with Me after Holy Communion. You may even want to take a few minutes to share a prayer with Me in front of My Tabernacle before you leave. The important message is to live your faith throughout the whole week. Your religious concerns are not just for Sunday only. I am at your side every moment, so seek My help at any time. By giving Me reverence at Mass and listening to My Spirit, you can have the joy of My love extend through everyone present. Share this peace of Mine with those around you, and My love will permeate everything you do."**

**Saturday, July 11, 1998:** (St. Benedict)
At St. Thomas More Church, Denver, Co. after Communion I could see a triangle with a goat figure in the middle and a light shone brightly on this image. Jesus said: **"My people, beware of the lies and seeming miracles of the Antichrist among you. Whenever someone comes in My Name, do not believe them. The evil one will come as a man of peace and he will have superhuman powers. Do not take the Mark of the Beast and do not worship him in any way. Call on My help and that of your guardian angel and I will protect you from the Antichrist. He will come at a time of chaos, but his reign will be a tyranny of evil where My faithful will be persecuted. Avoid his influence by going into hiding and trust in My food and My help. He will have an evil charisma and an attraction in his words to try and steal souls from Me. Keep focused on My love and I will provide you with all of your needs. The Antichrist's reign will be**

brief as I will crush his power and cast these evil ones into Hell. Do everything with My power to warn others not to believe in this man of lies and evil worship."

Later, at St. Thomas More Adoration, Denver, Co., I could see a children's cartoon show with some large yellow forms falling down. Jesus said: "My people, be careful what TV programs your children are watching. Some of these programs form little minds into things they should not be viewing. Some cartoons advocate violence and teach the wrong morals to the children. They are vulnerable to subliminal messages and even sudden flashes of light that can cause seizures. The TV programming is a weapon of the Antichrist in trying to control your minds. It would be better to not have your children watch TV, so they can develop their skills without useless distractions. Spend your time teaching your children the Faith, instead of leaving them to be influenced by an evil babysitter. Your time to teach the children is too short, so ask My help in teaching them properly of their Catholic heritage."

**Sunday, July 12, 1998:**
At Mother Cabrini's Shrine in Colorado, after Communion, I could see Mother Cabrini dressed in black. She said: **"Thank you, my children, for coming to my shrine to share my love with all of you at Mass. The reading of the Good Samaritan Gospel is near and dear to my heart. As Jesus used this story to describe neighborly love, I offer my life of service up to all of you as an example of love of neighbor as well. Jesus' command, to go out and do the same, is the same plea that He gives to all of you. You cannot stand by and do nothing when your neighbor needs your help. Your neighbor has both spiritual and physical needs that you should see and help them without being asked. All that you do now may seem insignificant, but in the eyes of God they are spiritual treasures that He will store up for you. Do not come to your judgment with empty hands, but bring all of your works of mercy to God, Who sees everything."**

Later, at St. Thomas More Adoration Denver, Co., I could see an ornate vision of Jesus being born in Bethlehem. Jesus said: **"My people, I am showing you My First Coming because you need to** know the details of My birth before you can understand My Second Coming. The myrrh represents the suffering which you will have to endure during the tribulation as I suffered on Calvary. The frankincense is to give glory to My Kingship in how My Triumph will reign over the earth as Satan and his demons are chained in Hell. The gold represents the beautiful gleaming walls of the new Jerusalem as it is lowered to the earth. All of the gifts of the wise kings were a royal foretelling of My Era of Peace that I will share with My faithful. Give glory and praise to My Second Coming as the angels first greeted Me on the first Christmas. As the Wise Men shared their gifts with Me, I am asking My messengers to share My gift of knowledge. Give hope to My people of how I will soon reign over all the earth in triumph."

**Monday, July 13, 1998:**

At St. Thomas More in Denver, Co., after Communion, I could see a beautiful house against a beautiful view of nature. Jesus said: "My people, when you look upon My creation, see how beautiful and splendid it is to the eye. Everything in creation is good in and of itself. You, My people, are a part of My creation and you all are special because of your souls and their immortality. Even though man is created beautifully with free will, you are weak because of the corruption of Adam's sin. Man has polluted the earth both physically and spiritually because of the presence of evil. My faithful have been gifted to understand this battle of good and evil. Keep your focus on Me and follow My commands and you will reach your destination in Heaven. Do not let money, pride or greed for possessions and power disturb your peace with Me. All of these earthly things are the influence of evil. Worship only Me and none of the idols of Earth. Do not corrupt My pure creation with evil, but build up My True Church bringing souls to love Me."

**Tuesday, July 14, 1998:**

At St. Stephen's Church, Glenwood Springs, Co. after Communion I could see an ornate church with gold trim. Jesus said: "My people, your modern churches give very little reverence to Me. Why are you so afraid to place My Cross of Crucifixion on your altars? Why do you place My Blessed Sacrament away from My people? You would do better to renovate your faith in your hearts than your desecration of My altars. In your older churches, it was more uplifting with the reverence to the saints and angels. Your new churches are barren of any holy life. Give the people a closeness to Heaven by showing them role models in the saints. Place My Presence back into the same room of worship with the people. Put My holiness before the people so they can worship Me, instead of man's importance. The lack of reverence in not displaying the pictures and statues of the saints shows a weak faith and sends the wrong message to the little children. Your faith could grow stronger by giving better witness of holiness to the people. Respect for My Real Presence will wane if My priests do not cultivate this respect by their example. The sense of the sacred is missing in your barren new churches. You would be better to follow the lessons of previous generations in the old churches."

Later, at St. Benedict's Monastery, Snowmass, Co., before the tabernacle I could see an open door to let some fresh air in. Jesus said: "My people, you need to let some fresh air in on your faith and in your churches. Call on the help of the Holy Spirit to make you humble and slow down your lives. You have become too sophisticated in your technologies and you would be better off with simple lives. It is not necessary to have expensive and exotic homes and cars. Many times you center too much of your lives on gathering these possessions. Come to Me in the quiet of your heart and you will see how you can be satisfied with little in earthly things, yet be rich in spiritual blessings. When you spend your time working for My Will, it will always gain you more merits than working for your own selfish goals. So, be satisfied with My Presence in My Sacraments and that will be enough for your soul."

**Wednesday, July 15, 1998:**

At St. Stephen's Church, Glenwood Springs, Co., after Communion, I could see a lectionary book on a pedestal at Mass. Jesus said: "My people, look to My Scriptures as My Revelation for your example how to live your lives. The Holy Spirit has inspired the writers of My Scripture, as I have inspired the saints and prophets to do My Will. Rely on My Church in its teachings for a proper interpretation of My Scriptures. There are beautiful lessons in life in both My Old and New Testament. The people of past days had little in the way of your comforts, yet they succeeded still in being saints. See in the Gospel how I do confuse the proud and the learned to humble them so they do not get puffed up with their pride. I call on you many times to come to Me in the innocence of children. It is in the simple life that you will see to put away the cares of the world and be focused on following My Will. Open your heart to Me so I can enter it and show you how to live in My Divine Will."

Later, at St. Thomas More Adoration, Denver, Co., I could see various levels of Heaven indicated by clouds. There were streaks of lightening between the clouds separating each Heaven. Jesus said: "My people, you are seeing the various separations of the levels of Heaven indicated by the increasing height of the layers of clouds. All of you are judged by your faith and good works to which level is befitting your destination. Strive, My people, to follow My Will as perfectly as possible to be members of My Heavenly Family. Even if you are gifted with faith, you must keep humble in your prayer life, since all of you are sinners and in need of repentance. Keeping holy each day is your goal. By living My Divine Will and cleansing your sins, you will be a part of My faithful, calling souls to Me. Do not worry about the evil ones around you. My grace will cast them into Hell. Live only to please Me by remaining true to your consecration to Me."

**Thursday, July 16, 1998:**

At St. Thomas More Church, Denver, Co., after Communion, I could see a large cave opening shaped like a hangar and then a light shown into the cave. Jesus said: "My people, in life there are many challenges and disappointments. You may have to endure difficulties, but it is all part of carrying your cross on earth. You may be persecuted and tested in this coming Tribulation, but do not worry because I will be watching over you. Your worrying cannot change things beyond your control, so accept your inconveniences gracefully. The light shining into the opening is a witness to My glory that will overcome everything. Have faith in My help and protection and everything will be provided for you. I will provide a safe haven for those who are faithful and trusting in My Word. Those who are faithful will live in the Era of Peace as a reward for following My Will. When you see the beauty and bountifulness of this new land, you will wonder why you ever worried at all about the outcome of your life. Hold firm in your belief of My promises and you will be consoled in your salvation."

Later, at the prayer group, I could see the front row of a set of desks in a school room. I asked if Thomas could speak to me. He said: "Thank you for receiving me. I felt uneasy that I could not go on in school, since I was taken so soon in life. I was happy to have a few years to share with my fellow students who were with me all the way. I share my love especially with my family for their support in this hard experience. Please pray for me as I pray for you."

I could see a crossroads in two main streets and it represented the choice we have in life. Jesus said: "My people, in every life you are faced with the same decision that each person must make. You have a choice between the broad highway to Hell or the narrow road to Heaven. For you it may seem impossible at times to reach Heaven, but with My help, all that is impossible becomes possible. Come to Me and take My yoke upon you for it is easy and My burden is light."

I could see some old cement footings of a torn down building and many of these sights were around our country. Jesus said: "My people, look around at your factory jobs disappearing, as your buildings begin to rot. You are seeing the self-destruction of your industrial might. The One World financiers are pillaging your country of its most important wealth and that is its people. The laws and favored agreements that your leaders were allowed to make, have enabled your employers to trade your jobs for cheaper ones with no concern for their workers. The greed for money and earnings in your stock market will be your ruination. Your greed will fall in on you as your financial empire will collapse under the weight of its own sins."

I could see some beautiful scenes with rivers and mountains. Jesus said: "**My people, take a closer look at the beauty of My creation all around you. Sometimes when you are on vacation, you can appreciate coming close to nature. Life is not just your race for survival in your cities. You need to see the whole world in its entirety to appreciate the glory of My creation. Give thanks to Me for all the gifts and blessings that I have bestowed upon your country. It is because you do not fully realize all of My gifts, that you will fall in your sins. Know that I am the one for you to worship because I have given you everything. All that you are and have comes from Me. So, give Me praise and glory and give Me all the credit for what you accomplish.**"

I could see some mines where gold was brought out. Jesus said: "**My people, there is a desire in some people to get rich quick. Whether it be in striking a rich vein of gold, making money in the stock market, or winning the lotto, these have become obsessions for some. Money has caused much sin by people's greed, even to steal from others. There is more to life than being rich. Adam and Eve were cast from the Garden to earn their bread by the sweat of their brow. Your suffering here is a test of your faith in Me. You are here to serve Me and not just your own selfishness. Look to the Heaven that awaits My faithful, and that will be your most desired treasure.**"

### Friday, July 17, 1998:

After Communion, I could see a small animal prostrate and dying from the heat. Jesus said: "**My people, I am showing you that the heat and the drought will continue to test your people. All of these things will test your food supplies as the great famine will test your world. All of humanity will feel the effects of these food losses as I will continue to bring you to your knees in prayer. Your weather events and your wars will become a major threat to your survival. It will be these reasons that will set the stage for the Antichrist to assume power. Prepare now with food and prayer for the many trials that man will have to suffer. You will have to seek My help for both your spiritual and physical survival. Those that are faithful I will protect, but many souls will be persecuted for My Name's sake.**"

Later, at Adoration, I could see some people behind bars in a prison. Jesus said: **"My people, there will be many people seeking My help when the devil and his angels will try to win the world over to their domination. There will be a cleansing of all religious people and those defending their country's freedoms. If freedoms are not fought for, then your freedoms will dissipate into nothing. The New World Order people will think they can control the whole world, but they will see conquering the free will and spirit of each person is more of a task. This clash of good and evil will take on a new perspective such that souls will be challenged to live their faith. You can only obtain freedom by your struggling against evil with My grace. Without Me, you are nothing and Satan would sift you. But I will not allow him to conquer you, only to test your endurance. When you fight for My heralding of a new Era of Peace, then you will witness the power of My glory."**

**Saturday, July 18, 1998:**

After Communion, I could see a lot of tombs where people were buried. The tombs were vertical slits open for those souls to be resurrected. Jesus said: **"My people, I am showing you the tombs of those who will be martyred for My Name's sake during the Tribulation. These are the souls who will refuse to take the Mark of the Beast, nor worship him. They will be raised up again with glorified bodies to live in the Era of Peace. Those who knowingly take the Mark of the Beast and worship the Antichrist will envy the dead. They will be tortured with fire, scorpions, and plagues, but they will not die yet. These are the ones who will wish the mountains would fall on them, because they will suffer a hell on earth. At My Coming they will be chained in Hell never to leave their punishment. The faithful I will protect as I greet them all into the Era of Peace. Those who would give their lives up to Me will save their lives."**

Later, at Holy Name Nocturnal Adoration I could see an A frame house. Jesus said: **"My people, this sign represents My kingship over everything from alpha to omega or a to z. Your house is where the heart is and where you put down your roots to live. Some may be more mobile than other families, but home** is where you gravitate for peace and rest. No matter how humble it may appear, one's home is a special place. In the next life, your real home will be in Heaven and you will not want to be anywhere else. Give praise and glory to Me who grants your requests. When My faithful come to My Judgment Gates, I will call on all of you to accept My Will over your own forever. Be thankful for your gift of faith and the opportunity to come to Me for your salvation."

Sunday, July 19, 1998:

After Communion, I could see a separation of light between the darkness of space and the light of the sun striking the earth. Jesus said: **"My people, you need to see the big picture of life and death to understand today's Gospel about Martha and Mary. You have the things to eat and your comforts about you, but life in the spirit is everlasting and more important than the life of the body. You sometimes worry too much about what you will eat and what you will wear. I feed the birds of the air and I clothe the lilies of the field. Would I not care for you more who are worth more than a flock of sparrows? Faith and trust in Me and My Words are all that you need. I will provide for all of your needs if you seek Me first. Mary's portion was to love Me and listen to My Words of life and she was not denied her desire. Caring for people's needs is also your duty, but your priorities must find that serving Me is the most important. For the things of earth pass away tomorrow, but I offer you eternal life."**

Later, at Adoration, I could see a lot of cattle being herded and then another scene of only one skinny longhorn. Jesus said: **"My people, as this drought continues, many livestock will be at risk as well as people. Unless there is special care for man and beast, there will be more deaths involved. Water may have to be rationed both to the city dwellers as well as the farmers. Again the threat of loss of life in the coming famine will spread as food and water become scarce. Now is the time to store food and water before it will be too late. As more events take place, you will see your food supplies at risk and managing what is available could cause problems in distribution. As people feel threatened for food, a chaos will result giving the Antichrist** and the One World people a chance to control the world's population. Beware when your food supplies are manipulated, since those controlling the food will be your masters. Fear not, for a time is coming when I will need to provide you food by multiplication in order for you to survive. Trust in Me even when it may be impossible by earthly standards."

Monday, July 20, 1998:
After Communion, I could see a large cross and it stood in a dark cave. Jesus said: "My people, the age I lived in and the present age are alike in that they both want signs of what is to come. Through My prophets I have given you many prophecies and these have been fulfilled and still many do not believe. Those that ask for signs are those who are blind by a lack of faith in Me. For if true believers saw My miracles or today saw the many signs of the End Times, they believed. It is only those who do not believe in My Word and do not accept miracles that fail to believe in Me or the signs I perform. I died on the cross for all of you so you could one day be resurrected with Me in Heaven. Keep focused on Me throughout your life as you carry your cross. This life is very short and those who believe in Me, even without signs, will receive a just reward with Me. You all will have to die with Me one day and suffer the insult of being buried in the bowels of the earth. But your vindication will be when I resurrect all of My faithful to enjoy eternity in the joy and peace of Heaven."

Later, at Adoration, I could see a proud goat with large horns. On the other side there were lambs being joined together. Jesus said: "My people, look on this scene as a representation of the battle of good and evil. I will separate the goats from the lambs as I will separate My faithful from this evil lot. The goats represent the proud and the arrogant who place their trust in money and power rather than Me. The lambs represent My faithful who are set out and are tormented by wolves in sheep's clothing. Those who are loving Me and their neighbor I will gather into My fold. For you are the innocent ones who follow My Voice of Truth. But for those who seek only earthly pleasures and comforts these are the lukewarm I will cast out of

My mouth. I pursue every soul to their dying day as My lost sheep. But if you refuse to love Me and accept My Will, My Justice will cast this evil lot into the eternal abyss of Hell. Do everything you can with My help to bring these lost souls to love Me. Explain to them that eternal love with Me far surpasses the eternal hate of Satan."

Tuesday, July 21, 1998:

After Communion, I could see a large dove representing the Holy Spirit. I asked if the Holy Spirit could speak and He said: "I am the Spirit of Love and I come in this year declared for Me by your Pope. Continue to request My help in your work of evangelization of the Gospel. It is the spiritual power that you need in fighting Satan and his angels. You are dealing with principalities and powers beyond your capability to fight. So, call on your heavenly helpers in Me, the angels, and the saints. We are all here to answer your requests for protection. For in the trials that you will face, I will be the One to speak through your lips and I will give you the grace and strength to endure this battle. Even if you must suffer and die for Jesus, I will be at your side to sustain you. Never fear the powers of evil, when you have Me to support you. Follow the Will of God in your mission and you all will find your peace with God in Heaven."

Later, at Our Lady of Peace Adoration, Canton, Ohio, I could see a gravestone and then a cave going into the ground. I then saw a chariot moving, but it became engulfed in flames. Jesus said: "My people, during the Tribulation you will see some martyred for My Name's sake, as a religious persecution will come over your land. I am showing you the caves deep in the earth where you will find hiding places from the Antichrist. There will be springs of healing waters both for drinking and to heal your sicknesses. I will provide food and water for you miraculously, just as I did for My people in the desert in the Exodus. When you see the chariots burning, it is a symbol for you that My angels will keep you from harm. The evil men will not be able to reach you, no matter how sophisticated their devices are. My angels will wrap their arms of protection around you, so even the demons will not be able to attack you. Have peace in your hearts without any fear or anxiety for these times. Everything will be provided for you to the least detail."

**Wednesday, July 22, 1998:**
At the Knights of Columbus Hall in Akron, Ohio, I could see some priests on an altar and all the people were dressed in black. They were all in sackcloth and ashes. Jesus said: **"My people, I have told you many times that the only sign that I will give this generation is the sign of Jonah.** He went to Nineveh declaring that city would be destroyed in forty days if they did not repent of their sins. You, America, are also being called in the same way. A symbolic forty days is your sentence as well. Unless your country repents of its sin, you also will fall in ruin. You are still committing sins of abortion and sins of the flesh. I have warned you repeatedly to stop your sins and repent. Seek My forgiveness in Confession. Your time of judgment draws near. The chastisements, that have visited you, are to bring you to your knees. Prepare now for My Second Coming by purifying your soul by My Sacraments. Those who are not properly prepared with the white wedding garments will be cast outside to wail and gnash their teeth. Now is the acceptable time to seek your salvation by coming to Me in faith. Those who do not accept Me and follow My Will will suffer forever in Hell. Come to Me out of love or come to Me from the fear of punishment in Hell, but come however you can."**

Later, at Our Lady of Peace Adoration, Canton, Ohio, I could see a large gold plated holy water font in a new church. Jesus said: **"My people, many of your new churches are too modern and devoid of a feeling of holiness. This golden water font is an example of how you spend too much money on things that are not as important as the statues and the stations that are missing. Do not let your church architects be so taken up with prizes for an impressive structure. Concern yourselves with a church that fits My purpose rather than one that fits man's fancy. You are building your churches and remodeling older churches to look cold with no love on the walls. You need to show statues that remind the people of Me, the saints or My mother. Without these images, there are no role models to show your chil-**

dren. Witness to My love also with a proper Crucifix showing My Suffering on the Cross. I died for all of mankind and you need to remind your people of this self-giving gift of My life for your sins. All of these devotions that give reverence to My Real Presence are necessary to show you how much I love you. It is My Sacramental Presence in the Eucharist that is calling for your praise and your glory."

**Thursday, July 23, 1998:**

At Massillon, Ohio, I could see some sacred vessels holding the Eucharist. Jesus said: **"My people, I have shown you before that you may have to protect and preserve My Blessed Sacrament. Remember how I told you that I will remain with you until the end of time. I will be with you present in My Host even through the Tribulation. Give Me honor and reverence for My Real Presence. This Transubstantiation of the bread and wine into My Body and Blood is My most precious gift that I can give of Myself to you. Treasure My Presence since this is your little piece of Heaven that I share with you at every valid Mass. I love you with an infinite love and I share this love most perfectly with you in Holy Communion. Even when you cannot receive Me in a Mass, you can call on Me in Spiritual Communion at any time. While you still have My Presence with you, visit Me often in the Tabernacle or at perpetual adoration. Encourage others to make special visits with Me as well. Remember to always give Me reverence and I will witness for you before My Father in Heaven."**

Later, at the prayer group, I could see a long line of beautiful pictures displayed for the faithful. Jesus said: **"I thank Irena for all of your many hours of love which go into making your pictures. They will continue to share your love with the reverence given to My mother and all of those represented in the pictures. They are a treasure of love beyond a price in your worldly goods. Continue in your work for your reward is in Heaven."**\*

I could see some large statues in a church. There were holes on the side so they could be carried off in haste. Jesus said: **"My**

---

\* Irena decorates icons and pictures with great beauty.

Josyp Terelya
1998

people, a time is coming when all of the statues and icons will be in danger of being desecrated. An evil spirit will touch the hearts of evil men to desire to destroy all that is holy or the witnesses to those of Heaven. This religious persecution will empty your churches and threaten all of the lives of My faithful. Pray much that you will be strengthened by My help to endure this tribulation."

I could see a man and his shirt was torn from him and his scapular and crucifix could be seen. Jesus said: **"My people, I am asking you to wear your sacramentals. Especially wear My mother's Scapular and My Crucifix. You are consecrating your-**

selves and your actions to us by your being faithful to your promises. Your Blessed Sacramentals will protect you from evil spirits in your trial. Have faith and hope in Me that My mother's mantle and My arms will wrap our protection around your souls. Have faith in praying for your relatives' souls as they will be spared My justice for your sake."

I could see some glimmering walls shine a beautiful light among the whole building which was on the site of holy ground for the Tribulation. Our Lady came dressed in a beautiful dress sparkling with jewels. Mary said: "**My dear children, I thank you for your many Rosaries and all of your devotions to me. My visits will be few in number, since my purpose has been accomplished in preparing my children to greet my Son when He comes. Have faith and trust in My Son's healing hand during the trial. I am showing you the miraculous graces that will be poured out on all those who are drawn to my shrines, especially during the Tribulation. Follow your angels to my holy places and all of your needs will be satisfied.**"

I could see an older vehicle over fifteen years old. Jesus said: "**My people, your older vehicles will be safer in bringing you to My safe havens. Newer vehicles will only be useful for part of your travel to your refuge destination. Do not have fear or worry in how you will be protected. It is only your concern to remain faithful to Me and follow My Will. All of My faithful will join Me in My Era of Peace, whether you are martyred or not. Do not fear martyrdom, for I will soften your pain and give you a grace to endure it.**"

I could see some lambs being offered in sacrifice on a stone altar. Jesus said: "**My people, I have refrained from telling you of how many souls will have to suffer martyrdom for My Name's sake. It is enough to say that it will be more than a few. But each death is a witness in faith to those unbelievers. It is hard for some to understand that many love Me even if they have to give their lives up for Me. When I died for you, I did so willingly because I was sent to redeem your souls. I had a price to pay to witness My sincere love for all of you. So, when you may be faced with a possible decision between loving Me or keeping your life, think of how I died for you. Remember also that in** order to save your souls, you will have to die to yourself. Desire Heaven more than staying in this evil world."

I could see a reflection of a monstrance and Host in a mirror image in water. Jesus said: **"My people, when you look on My Consecrated Host, this is a reflection of My love and My Spirit present in the Sacred Host. Just as each one of you are made to My image, each Consecrated Host is a mirror image of My likeness. When you come before My Blessed Sacrament, think of the image of My Face on the shroud, because each host represents My sacrifice on the altar of My life for you."**

**Friday, July 24, 1998:**

After Communion, I could see a ship at sea and there was a misty rose over the ship as it was being guided. Jesus said: **"My people, I am showing you My Church as a ship on its way to the destination of Heaven. I am the rose that guards My Church and I am at the helm directing your course. Those who follow My Pope John Paul II will have nothing to fear, for He is My representative leading My Church. Listen to his words and follow him because he is inspired with the Holy Spirit. There will come a time, My people, when an Antipope will try to take control of My Church. I am asking you in those days to stay the course of My faithful remnant. Never deviate from the teachings of My Apostles. This apostate will be an imposter pope and he will be a shepherd on the outside, but a ravenous wolf on the inside. All of My faithful laity and clergy must refuse to follow this false witness who will try to destroy My Church from within. He will blaspheme Me by worshiping the Antichrist. Do not follow this evil pope, but only follow the teachings I have placed before you. Those who listen to My voice and follow My commands will reach their desired destination in Heaven."**

**Saturday, July 25, 1998:** (St. James)

After Communion, I could see some kneelers for Adoration of God. Jesus said: **"My people, remember that you are here to serve and not be served. By your seeking fame and riches on this earth, you only seek to serve your own will. In reality, you all were created in My image to know, love and serve Me. When** you serve Me, you have to conform your will to following My Divine Will. Do not let your pride run your life, because fame and fortune are fleeting in this life. Instead, look for ways to please Me and help your neighbor. In that way you are building up treasures in Heaven that will last forever. When you seek heavenly things you will find a lasting peace instead of a momentary pleasure on earth."

Sunday, July 26, 1998:

After Communion, I could see someone in a daze at church. Jesus said: "My people, when you come to Mass, do not just go through the motions, but participate with your heart. When you come to Mass, raise up your spirit and keep fixed on My message in the readings. Remove all of your daily distractions and see the true purpose that you have in life of serving Me. When the fish swim upstream to spawn, you likewise need to swim upstream to your goal in Heaven. If you do not struggle in carrying your cross, you will get carried downstream by the current of the world's desires. Those who are lukewarm are lifeless in My eyes because they are neither hot nor cold. To win your eternal salvation you must strive to follow My Will and die to self. Put a spirit of My love in your step and live your faith as if you believe in it for all that you do."

Later, at Adoration, I could see an old house in the city and then I saw a car with a man in it start down a steep hill in the city. Jesus said: "My people, your cities will grow poorer while those in the suburbs will grow richer. As time goes on there will be a gulf of discontent for those in the city seeing their jobs flow to the suburbs. This will set the stage for a class struggle that could cause riots in your streets once again. These problems will combine with the famine and weather problems to set the time of the Antichrist in position for takeover. Know that your riches will be stripped from you by both a financial crisis and physical stealing and looting. This chaos in your streets will allow the Antichrist to assume power in the name of peace. People will trust this seeming man of peace to bring stability back into their lives. But by his lies and miracles, the people will enable the Antichrist to control the whole world briefly. I will shorten the Antichrist's reign as I chain him in Hell. I will restore real peace and a new Jerusalem on the earth. Be joyous that this reign of evil will be short-lived and only a test of your endurance for a time. My victory is assured, so do not worry about the tyranny of this false witness."

Monday, July 27, 1998:

After Communion, I could see some doors opening in space as a satellite was being set into orbit. Jesus said: "My people, this is a strange satellite that you see being placed in orbit. It has an unusual shape because its mission is one of lights and mirrors. This is an orchestrated attempt to help the Antichrist show signs and wonders in the vast expanse of space. With these satellites and the lasers in proper position, a light show can be produced to dazzle all of the Antichrist's subjects on earth. These subjects will give praise to the Antichrist for performing such miraculous lights. These lights will shine in large designs which no one has ever witnessed before, but in fact they will only be dramatic illusions. Do not believe in his magical appearances or give him worship. I will soon come in triumph to defeat all of these evil men and evil spirits. I will remove them from the earth and cast them into Hell and they will no longer cause evil on the earth. Rejoice for soon My faithful will be enjoying their place in My Era of Peace."

Later, at church, I could see an older ornate church. Jesus said: "My people, I love all of My children very much for wherever you are in your faith. Those who have a special reverence for My Real Presence have a special place in My heart as well. Those faithful of years gone by had a special reverence in the churches they built for Me. Today's churches are colder because man appears to be making these modern churches more for his glory than Mine. In older days the saints and My Presence were of more importance. Today, you place My Real Presence on the side or in other rooms from the main body. Little by little My priests have let My faithful down by not teaching about My Real Presence. Is there any surprise that few believe that I am really Present in My Consecrated Host? There is an evil influence which is trying to remove all that is sacred in My

**Church. Pray, My people, to restore holiness to My Church and not to minimize it.** Continue My heritage of love in My sacraments so your future generations can share in the love that My faithful have for Me."

Tuesday, July 28, 1998:

After Communion, I could see a tiered waterfall to cleanse a baby being baptized. Then the waterfall stopped flowing. Jesus said: **"My people, you began your Christian life by having the cleansing waters of Baptism wash away your original sin from Adam. This first step in faith was provided for you by your parents and godparents. As you advanced in age, you have had to repeat these early vows to renounce Satan and give glory and praise to Me for My graces to you. As you grew up, the weakness to sin has tarnished the innocence of your youth. The desires and influence of the worldly concerns soon corrupts your soul. That is why from time to time, you need to seek My cleansing waters of grace in Confession, so your sins can be washed away. When the waterfall stopped, it was because of your offenses against Me. But when you return to My Sacrament of Reconciliation, that waterfall of My graces is turned on once again. When you take a bath each day to wash away the dirt and sweat of the day, think also of Confession as your opportunity to cleanse your soul of the dirt of sin. Then you will once again be clean and innocent as the Baptism of a newborn. It is your responsibility to keep your soul clean by avoiding sin. But if you should fall, My grace of forgiveness is always there for your asking."**

Later, before the Blessed Sacrament I could see an opened Bible and there was a black lace that spread all over the pages. Jesus said: **"My people, I am showing you that this evil age is upon you and the evil one is spewing his hatred upon mankind. You are living the last book of My Revelation as the Antichrist is about to assume his brief reign. You are seeing people coming forth to deny My Scriptures. Others are worshiping many idols of the world. I am bringing this trial about you to test your faith. It is as I gave Job many blessings and I tested him by taking them away. So it is with My faithful. I will be testing you by stripping you of** your possessions as well. Evil ones will come to persecute you and you may even have to endure torture or martyrdom for My Name's sake. Your test comes in realizing that you cannot endure this trial on your own. When you call on My help, I will then know how much you trust in My protection of your soul. For with My miraculous gifts and the help of your angels, all of My faithful will come through this Tribulation to enjoy My victory in the Era of Peace. I am telling you the outcome, so there is no reason to fear the power of evil. My power reigns supreme and nothing happens without My willing it so. So take courage, My children, in the test of your faith, but rejoice in the knowledge that you will share in the joy of your Master."

**Wednesday, July 29, 1998:** (St. Martha)

After Communion, I could see some women being embarrassed for their sexual sins. Jesus said: **"My people, why have many of your women today lost their sense of shame in their sins of sexual pleasure? Your society's morals have reached a low ebb by all of your movies and financial exploitation of women. But it is the women's consent that allows this sinful activity to continue. By living with men unmarried and selling their bodies, women have placed themselves in continual occasions of sin. These lifestyles can lead these women to a road to Hell for their sins. The men are as much to blame for continuing these relationships and they are headed for the same end as well. It is good to have models for living a good Christian life and St. Martha is there for young women. Follow her example in helping others rather than being so concerned over selfish pleasure. Do not place yourselves in such occasions of sin or you could lose your souls to Satan. It is better to reserve your gift of sex until after marriage, where your union can be blessed by My grace. This marriage act was reserved as a gift of love for the spouses rather than a cheapened moment of selfish lust. For those who have bad habits of sex, you need to pray for self-control of your passions and go to frequent Confession to have these sins forgiven. Do not be lazy in your sins of pleasure, but strive to imitate the saints, who have reached great heights in Heaven by following My Will instead of their own."**

**Thursday, July 30, 1998:**

After Communion, I could see an altar with a door rounded at the top. I then saw an image of the two tablets of the Ten Commandments of the Old Testament, still with the altar in the foreground. Jesus said: **"My people, I am showing you your salvation into Heaven through My Sacrifice of the Mass. You know in the Old Testament how My people made sacrifices on the altar by the blood of animals. You remember how it was the Blood of the lamb painted on the lintels that saved My people from the Angel of Death in Egypt. So it is on your altars at each Mass. My blood is shed in an unbloody manner at each Mass to re-enact My dying on the cross for your sins. Without My Blood being poured out on each of you, your sins could not be cleansed. So keep this thought of My greatest sacrifice for all of you in mind when you see this at every Mass. It is My Real Presence before you that you are receiving in My Body and Blood under the appearances of bread and wine. Never let anyone tell you different, that it is the sacrifice of My Body and Blood which you witness at every Mass. Anyone, who denies this sacrifice and speaks of My Eucharist as only a meal, is deeply deceived by the evil one and is misleading you. Stay by My Church's foundation in its teachings and do not follow the modernism of the apostates."**

Later, at the prayer group, I saw a huge flame in the middle and around it were various objects. These included a jukebox, a movie reel, dollar signs and a pyramid with an eye over it. Jesus said: **"My people, this flame represents the attractions of the Antichrist. He is orchestrating mind control through movies, music and those seeking fame and fortune. Look to what he will be doing, for there will be no worship of God — only worship of himself. He will use all of your earthly attractions to desire to follow him. He will promise you anything at the cost of your soul. My faithful, do not give in to his temptations, lies and seeming miracles. Worship only the one true God, and your soul will be protected from all evil."**

I could see an image of the Titanic next to an image of Noah's Ark. Jesus said: **"My people, on the one hand, you are seeing man's handiwork and you know of your failures. On the other** side, you are seeing things directed by God and you know of their endurance. So it should be for all that you do and make. When I direct the builder, you know it will stand. Have faith in My help, even during the Tribulation."

I could see some beautiful art form designs and then they developed into pictures of modern day airplanes. Jesus said: "My people, man has evolved through many ideas and trials until he has developed flight. Yet look at the birds and how they were created for flight. Man prides himself about his inventions and his technology, but they are nothing before My power. Do not think that because of your creations, you no longer need My help. I have provided you the materials you fashion, the light and the oxygen by which you breathe, and the spirit of your very soul. Remember that you were created to serve Me and this earth is only your chance to prove your love for Me. Do not desire to be gods in yourselves as Satan tempted Adam, but come to your Lord, who will love you always and provide for your needs."

I could see floods flowing down some main streets and lightening putting out some power lines. Jesus said: "My people, how long will you see your material things fall away and still you do not understand your need for prayer? You are distracted by many things, but only heavenly things are what you should seek. Seek to praise Me and serve your neighbor. When you replace self-love with My love, I will shower you with many blessings. But when you worship your material things instead of Me, I will wipe all of them away. I am a jealous God and I seek your love. When you are drawn to those worldly things, I am showing you how futile that pursuit is when tomorrow they are gone."

I could look up and see a circle of saints and angels looking down on the events of the world. Jesus said: "My people, all of Heaven is wondering why I have not brought My hand of justice on the world by now. Yet it is by My mercy that you have this extra time to pray and convert your lives. My justice has been postponed for a while because of your prayers. See the value in your prayer that can stop wars and worse destruction. I am calling on all of humanity to prepare for this last onslaught of the evil one. You will endure your trial first, before I will destroy the evil doers and chain them in Hell. Continue your hope and trust in Me and you will rejoice at My triumph." I could see a car and there was a yellow flash. I then saw some fires all over the country. Jesus said: "My people, you can see the purging of fires from nature or you can cause the horrific fires of a man-made nuclear fire. The choice is in your hands, if you want peace or war. My mother and I have requested your many Rosaries to avert a world nuclear encounter. Mankind is on the brink of this disaster and only love can win this battle. My arms and My mother's mantle are protecting you now. Like Moses held his hands up to win the battle, you must hold up your hands in prayer to prevent this holocaust."

I could see some ice on some power lines and then a bright sun came out to melt the ice. Jesus said: "My people, you have endured many storms and hardships over the last few years, but are you learning anything from them? I have told you the connection between your chastisements and your sins. See how important it is to seek the forgiveness of your sins. It is for this reason of bringing you to your knees, that these hardships are a blessing to you. When you see how you can get along without your possessions, you will understand why following My Will is better for your soul."

**Friday, July 31, 1998:**

After Communion, I could see several baskets that held babies. Jesus said: "My people, let none of My prophets or messengers be disheartened, because of those that criticize you. Many of My prophets have been abused verbally and physically for bringing an unpopular message. They are proclaiming My Word to repent. It is those listening who do not want to be told to reform their sinful lives. It is those listening that do not want to hear of chastisements. These men and women, that I call to give My message, should not be criticized, for they are only carrying out their duty to Me. There are false witnesses present as well who must be discerned with prayer. But My true prophets have and will suffer as I did, because the people desire to keep their sinful lives. To be reminded of one's sins causes sinners to reject their accusers and that is why prophets are abused. Many cannot tolerate listening to the truth and it is easier to try and discredit those teaching the Gospel. But to all of My messengers, I tell you to keep proclaiming My Word, no matter what consequences may befall you. Those messengers who fail to deliver My message will have to answer to My justice. Those who do not heed My message through My messengers are at fault and also will pay for abusing them."

Later, I could see a table with some vessels on it. Jesus said: "My people, I call on all of My faithful to serve your neighbor in their need, because as you serve them, you are serving Me. You are My arms and legs to go forward and do good works. By helping your neighbor in your corporal works of mercy, you are giving good example to others how to live the life of a Christian. Some serve with deeds, but you can also serve by your prayers, fasting and giving up your pain for others. I was suffering in many ways through life as a witness to you how you could follow in My footsteps. I suffered loneliness, rejection, and even betrayal from My own Apostles. In physical pain I suffered the scourging, My crown of thorns, the weight of My cross, the nail marks, and the spear in My side. I gave up every last drop of blood for all of mankind for the redemption of your souls and the forgiveness of your sins. So, do not be afraid to take on suffering, but do not waste your pain and disappointments. Offer all of your trials up for the conversion of poor sinners. By your suffering you may help others to reach Heaven. Then you can see the blessing that I give in suffering so you can understand the benefits in winning souls to Me in Heaven."

**Sunday, August 2, 1998:**

At Sacred Heart Church Tampa, Florida, after Communion, I could see the publican and a pharisee at church. Jesus said: "My people, when you come to church, do not count your blessings in pride and say how much better you are than someone else. Instead, be thankful for all of your blessings and strike your breast as the publican as he sought forgiveness of his sins. Remember that he, who exults himself, will be humbled and he, who humbles himself, will be exulted. As in the Gospel, it is better to grow rich in Me, than rich for yourself. You need to share all that you have with My Church and your neighbors. Even help until it is of your substance and not just out of your excess. You are only stewards of this life's possessions, you are not owners. When you die, they will be passed on. So, deal with everything as I would use them, never being selfish, but always sharing all that you have. For when you give of what you have in this life, you will be storing up true treasures in Heaven that will be everlasting in your next life."

### Monday, August 3, 1998:

At St. Charles Borromeo Church, Port Charlotte, Florida, after Communion, I could see Jesus at the altar holding His hands up to the Father. Jesus said: **"My people, I welcome all of you to receive the Bread of Heaven. All of you are invited and I even search for all of My lost sheep. Even though My call goes out to everyone, there are still some who refuse to receive Me. As I fed the thousands in the Gospel, I offer to feed all of My faithful My Body and Blood in My Eucharist. To worthily receive Me in Holy Communion you must not have any mortal sin, but have them forgiven in Confession. If you are to come to Heaven, you must come through Me, because I have redeemed you by My Death on the Cross. When I feed you My Heavenly Bread, your soul will be fully satisfied in My peace. It is the spiritual fulfillment of My grace that draws your soul to Me. Your soul will never be at peace until you accept Me as your Savior. You may wander through the world seeking earthly things, but they will never satisfy your soul. Your souls can only have its rest in Me, so seek Me first and all else will be provided for you. Have faith and trust in Me only and your soul will be forever in spiritual ecstacy."**

### Tuesday, August 4, 1998:

At St. William's Church Naples, Florida, after Communion, I could see the door to the church was closed and the people were standing outside. Jesus said: **"My people, a time is coming when your churches will be barred from entry, as you will suffer a religious persecution. No longer will you be able to share Mass** openly in public. For a while you will have underground Masses, which you should prepare for even now. As the Tribulation proceeds, even a secret Mass will be hard to find. At that time, you may call on Me and I will have your guardian angels deliver My Host on your tongue in Spiritual Communion. You will need your sacramentals of Rosaries, Holy Water and your Bibles. These are your treasures to take with you into hiding away from the evil of the Antichrist. Prepare for this testing of the Tribulation. You do not always appreciate the gifts that I give you in My Real Presence in My Eucharist. I will be with you to the end, but you will have to suffer much for My Name's sake. Pray for spiritual strength to endure this coming trial. My miraculous gifts will support your soul as long as you remain faithful to following My Will. Do not have fear, as St. Peter sank in the water, but have hope and trust in Me that I will care for you in all of your trials."

Later, at Adoration, I could see an old brown fighter from World War II fly into the water. Jesus said: "My people, as you have advanced in your technology, you are now more and more of a threat to your own survival. The proliferation of your nuclear weapons, new laser technology and your biological weapons are all a means of mass destruction that could wipe out parts of mankind. In the hands of terrorists or desperate people, these weapons could cause serious problems for man's very existence. So pray, My people, for peace in your world, so that these weapons will not be used. You have a dangerous balance of power that could be upset from many hot spots around the world. Seek the love of My peace and you will one day enjoy My Era of Peace, after I do away with all evil and all of these dangerous armaments. Without My intervention, man could destroy himself, but I will come soon to chain these evil men in Hell."

**Wednesday, August 5, 1998:** (Mary Major Church)
After Communion, I could see Mary in brown kneeling in meditation. Mary said: "My dear children, miracles play a large role in your lives whether they be big ones or small ones. You have seen how miracles were a major part of my Son's ministry on earth. He went from satisfying my request for the wine to bringing

Lazarus back from the dead. Each miracle showed the compassion that Jesus had for reaching out to help people. There have been many miracles throughout history even at my apparitions that went from springs of water appearing to miracles of the sun. All of these miracles were shared by Heaven to witness supernatural events and to help support the faith of my children. There are many little miracles of healing going on even in your day. There is more joy in an unexpected miracle than thinking miracles should happen when you want it to happen. So, rejoice when Heaven answers your prayers in miracles. Give thanks for these gifts without expecting them every time you want a request answered. The joy of Heaven is shared with you every day and these little touches help you on your road to Heaven."

Later, at Adoration, I could see a male nurse in a hospital. Jesus said: **"My people, your medical system will soon start to adopt the same ways of Germany during World War II. The authorities are trying to give you personal ID's so they can know your age and your religious background. Initially, your value of life has already been lowered due to your abortion mentality. You are being made ready for mercy killing and this will be followed by elimination of the elderly and then the handicapped. This is how the genocide of the Jews was made acceptable as the gradualism of killing grew worse based on trying to make a pure race. These signs of eliminating those undesired by some are present in your own medicine. In order to stop this killing, you need to turn around your death culture promoted by your zero population groups. Once the value of life is considered an inalienable right, you can stop your abortions and return to a civilized society. If you fail to turn this fight for life around, you will forfeit your life to those who want to exterminate you. An hour is coming when I will come to stop this carnage and place all of these killers in Hell for their evil deeds. Rejoice when I bring My justice on the earth at last. You will not wait long for My return."**

**Thursday, August 6, 1998:** (Transfiguration)

After Communion, I could see Jesus on Mt. Tabor with two white figures on either side of Him. He revealed Himself in a glorified body. Jesus said: **"My people, this was a preview to My**

Apostles of My Resurrection. It showed them My true power and it gave them hope to see Moses and Elias alive once again. When they saw these great leaders of the chosen people, they saw the meaning later of how all men would one day be resurrected as well. This vision was so dazzling that St. Peter wanted it to last longer. This was the second time My Father witnessed to My glory among men. This was another sign to all doubters that I truly am the Son of God and not just a mere man. Give glory and praise to My Kingship over man as My Father com-

manded you to listen to My Words. **As I prepared My Apostles for My Resurrection, I am preparing your generation for My Coming again on the clouds."**

Later, at the prayer group, I could see Jesus in the tomb and there was a flash of light. Jesus said: **"My people, when I resurrected from the tomb, there was a flash of brilliant light which left My imprint on the shroud. It was at My Resurrection that I took on a glorified body which was dazzling white in appearance. This was the same appearance which was foretold in My Transfiguration. Many of My followers did not recognize Me at first, but as I called their names and broke bread with them, there I was revealed in their presence. All of My faithful will one day be resurrected in glorified bodies as well. This is the hope I give all of you in looking forward to being with Me in Heaven."**

I could see some military men in Iraq. Jesus said: **"My people, these military men are playing a deadly game of daring each other into action. By keeping a constant threat in these oil countries, your forces will be tied down in a foreign land. You are protecting these nations from war, but one miscalculation can cause war to break out. Pray for peace all over the world so war may be averted."**

I could see a bomb underneath a bridge. Jesus said: **"My people, it is just a matter of time before some terrorist bombs could ignite another problem war. Certain militants do not want peace, but are content to cause unrest to get their way. Greed and power are conflicting elements in your world. These continual acts of violence will contribute to the chaos that will allow the Antichrist to take control. The apathy and a lack of will to fight for freedoms will cause this so-called man of peace to gain popularity."**

I could see a beach and a cliff eroded by a major storm. Jesus said: **"My people, you will continue to see the escalation of storms that will ruin much property and threaten the loss of more lives. Those near the coast lands and rivers will be more at risk from water damage. Man is so stubborn to change his ways, that you will have to repeat the hardships that you have suffered. When you see the connection between your sins and** your lost blessings, you will see how your lives of sin will lead you to ruin."

I could see Mary huddling children into a safe haven so they would not be harmed by evil men. Mary said: "My dear children, take care that you prepare for the day when you will have to go into hiding from the Antichrist. I will help in shepherding my children to my safe havens. The angels will protect you at my true apparition sites, so come share the protection of my mantle from evil men and evil spirits. Keep your Sacramentals with you in your Rosaries and your Scapulars."

I could see some groups of nuns in one place where their joy was great in following Jesus. Jesus said: "My people, many beautiful orders of nuns are suffering for Me in different ways. Some that assist the sick and dying receive their joy in helping others. Other orders are contemplative and are offering their lives of prayer for sinners. The joy in the hearts of these blessed women is beyond any riches that this world could offer."

I could see a red house on top of some mountains. Jesus said: "My people, I am sharing with you that your new homes will be found in the mountains. As the Tribulation is about to begin, My angels will lead some of you to caves in the hills. If necessary, they will even carve them out of the rock for you. I will provide for your shelter and the protection of your souls. You will need full trust in My miraculous gifts of life to provide you food and water. Seek Me first and you will have everything given to you."

**Friday, August 7, 1998:**

After Communion, I could see a coat of arms on a shield. Jesus said: "My people, there are many small skirmishes going on in your world at any time. These small wars are based on many ethnic differences and sometimes even religious differences. Why is man so quick to take up arms for the least problem, instead of trying to compromise in peaceful discussions? Deep down in the hearts of these conflicts is a desire to rule over their neighbors. The greed for land and power over their fellow man drives many to take up arms in war. It is the leaders who are at fault that lead their people into war. But the people who follow such madness are at fault for going along with their directives. Each new war breeds more hatred for the killing and injustices that go on. It is better to pray for a peaceful settlement than to allow these wars to continue. If man cannot turn around his greed for power, he will suffer the consequences of even larger conflicts. Search for ways of peace or you will be doomed to repeat your mistakes in war which only breeds destruction. Do not let Satan stir up hate, but live in My peace."

### Saturday, August 8, 1998:

At St. Richard's Church, North Olmstead, Ohio, after Communion, I could see a door and I focused on the handle. Jesus said: "My people, I am showing you this door as the way to your heart. Some people are cold and leave this door closed to Me, even when I knock. My children, open your hearts to My love and love of your neighbor. When you take your selfish pride out of your heart, you make room for Me to enter. Without love in your heart, you cannot find Me. If you do many deeds and do not have love, you are nothing. Love is so much a part of life, that you cannot advance in your spirituality without it. So love Me and your neighbor and your salvation will be your reward. Love even your enemies and you will gain treasure in Heaven."

### Sunday, August 9, 1998:

At St. Elizabeth Ann Seton Church, Fort Wayne, Indiana, after Communion, I could see the back of many heads all around the Blessed Sacrament in the monstrance. Jesus said: "My people, I am asking you to take time out of your busy schedules to visit Me often in My Blessed Sacrament. I have given you a lifetime to worship and praise Me as My angels do at all times. You were made to serve Me and not the world. So come, bring everyone you can to make special visits to Me. Even when possible, encourage your priests to have My Blessed Sacrament exposed often and even in Perpetual Adoration. Also, encourage the children of all ages to come with you to give Me homage. You witnessed how the kings of the East visited Me, so you see that I am more than worthy to receive your homage as well. When you come to give Me praise and glory, you can give Me thanks as well for all you have been given. Give me your troubles and I will guide you. Listen for My Words of direction and I can show you how to follow My Will. You are not alone, so come into My Real Presence and I will provide for your needs. Have faith and trust in Me that I will lead all who follow Me to Heaven."

Later, at St. Elizabeth Ann Seton's Church, Fort Wayne, Indiana, before the Blessed Sacrament I could see a child's toy reflected off the screen of a television set. Jesus said: "**My people, you are looking at the biggest distraction that you have on earth in your televisions. There is some good programming, but the bulk is misleading My faithful to follow worldly things. It is better to minimize your viewing and limit it to an hour or less. Especially, the children are spending too much time getting brainwashed with the world's values. This device has a captivating influence on both children and adults. So, do not let it run your life. Instead of wasting precious time, spend more time in prayer and good deeds. You will see, the less you watch TV, the more good things you will have time to do. When the Tribulation approaches, as signaled by the warning, take your TVs out of your houses and do not be influenced by watching the Antichrist. By prioritizing your time for Me and less for the world, you will keep Me in focus on your way to Heaven.**"

**Monday, August 10, 1998:** (St. Lawrence)

At St. Joseph's Church, Fort Wayne, Indiana, after Communion, I could see a cross with Jesus hanging on it. There were various views shown of Jesus on the cross. Jesus said: "**My people, you know how I suffered on the cross for your sins. I was the first martyr for My own cause. You have seen martyrs for God in the Old Testament and those that came after Me. In the coming trial, you will see many martyrs once again for the Faith. I ask all of My faithful to be strong in their faith, even if one day you may be tested by offering your life for Me. Salvation in Heaven would be yours immediately for those martyred in the Faith. I will be at your side to defend you against any evil doers. Have no fear, but continue your unswerving faith in Me. All those** who die for Me will be comforted in their pain. Even if you are not called to martyrdom, you must remain strong in your faith ever witnessing to My love. It is your persistence in faith that I desire for each of your souls. With a constant focus on Me, you will never deviate from your path to Heaven. Share your love of Me with your neighbors so you will never be ashamed of following Me in public, even when your life may be at stake."

Later, at the airport chapel in Chicago, Illinois, I could see an elevator going up. Jesus said: "My people, the elevator mix up, you experienced, is the same problem with the world. Many are in a fast paced race of life, so they run to the first elevator available. The reality of life is that you need to understand the direction you are headed first. A road chosen in haste may not lead you to Heaven. This is why it is important to consider your priorities in life, so you can see if you are doing things more for the world or for Me. Once you are on the right road to Heaven, you still need to keep a watch that you do not get off too soon at the wrong detour. The desires of the world can distract you from your goal, if you are not focused on Me. By having a good prayer life, you can better follow the narrow road to Heaven, instead of being misled down the broad road to Hell." (In our rush to get to Mass on time, we took the first available elevator, but the wrong one.)

**Tuesday, August 11, 1998:** (St. Clare's Feast Day)

At the Poor Clare's Monastery, Belleview, Illinois, after Communion, I could see a large hall that gave honor to today's saint-St. Clare. Jesus said: "**My dear people, it is a glorious day to honor the saints that have gone before you. The saints are examples to you of how to follow My Will in simple faith. I give all of My faithful hope that one day, you could become saints as well. To be a saint, you do not need fame and great miracles to witness to all of mankind. Many become saints by a humble surrender of their wills to follow My Plan for their lives. You too, can become saints if you dedicate your lives to My service. Every day consecrate your hearts to Me, so you will seek to do everything for Me. I call on my future saints to a life of prayer, fasting, and good works. All that you do in secret, My Father will** repay you in His blessings. It is to this devotion of true faith that I call all of you to live. Give good example to all those around you and be an inspiration of holiness in all of your actions. By working each day to serve Me, your crown of salvation will await you in Heaven. All those who come to Heaven are declared saints in My eyes and all Heaven will celebrate your feast day, even though those on earth may never know of your fame in My eyes."

Later, at church, in Belleville, Illinois, I could see a woman contemplating in a pew next to a confessional. Jesus said: "My people, when you come to Me in Confession, you need to spend some time in contemplating your sins against Me. Do not come in haste, but think through all of My Commandments so you are properly prepared. Come with a contrite heart in sorrow for your offenses. Come to Me to cleanse your sins so your soul can be beautiful before Me once again. Do not hold back any sins, but humbly confess everything to the priest. You need frequent Confession to keep placing yourself back on the narrow road to Heaven. Do not fear Confession or lazily put off going, because you never know when I will call you home. Be like the wise virgins, who were prepared when the master came. By always being watchful through frequent Confession, your soul will be ready for My judgment. He who sins but does not seek My forgiveness, risks the fires of Gehenna. So come in love to enjoy the peace of your Master, when you receive the cleansing graces of My absolution of your sins."

**Wednesday, August 12, 1998:**

At Our Lady of the Snows' Shrine Belleville, Illinois, after Communion, I could see some cells and disease germs invading these cells. Jesus said: "My people, I am showing you how evil men will try to spread disease as a means of controlling populations. They will try to wipe out certain people that may threaten the New World Order. They will use food and medicines as a means to try and get people to worship the Antichrist. Those who worship the Antichrist and take the Mark of the Beast will receive controlled food and medicines. Do not take what the evil ones will control. Instead, My faithful ones, follow My angels to your places of protection, where you will find healing and My Heavenly Manna. Do not fear anything of the evil one, but trust in My protection. I will shield your souls from the evil ones. In a short time I will bring this evil lot to justice as all of them will be chained in Hell. My faithful will then enjoy My Era of Peace, as a reward for your faithfulness. So rejoice, for My victory will be coming shortly."

Later, at Adoration, I could see a long dirt highway under construction. Then there was a large patch of dirt where some major effects of an earthquake could be seen. Jesus said: **"My people, you have seen many serious earthquakes and this one (5.4) can lead to something larger. This road is on a dirt road and many refuges are on such roads. With all of your trials in the cities, your angels will lead you to places of rural settings. As these tribulations of earthquakes, fires and famines increase, so must your trust increase that I will lead you to safe places. Many will lose their possessions for My sake, but they will be blessed with many miraculous gifts that will far surpass anything you own. When you are guided to your refuges by your guardian angels, I will provide for your food and shelter. With Me providing for you, why should you have any fear? Trust in My Will and you will come to My Era of Peace. Rejoice that you are living in this age."**

### Thursday, August 13, 1998:

After Communion, I could see some tall pyramids moving in a row and they became smaller at the end of the line. Jesus said: **"My people, I am showing you how your leaders lord it over you in their riches. Those who are rich and famous will soon lose all that they have, because they have grown rich for themselves. The Antichrist and Satan will double cross them both on earth and in the next life. These evil men will have their positions usurped as the Antichrist will take over their power and and they will be eliminated. Even in the next life, their glory will go for nought as they are cast into Hell. So, do not be attracted by fame and riches, for this life is short and all of your possessions will be stripped from you. It is only when you share or give this wealth to others, that it will gain you any-**

thing in the next life. It will be harder for the rich to reach Heaven, because of their affluence and their little need of Me."

**Thursday, August 13, 1998:**
At the prayer group, I could see a skull and crossbones overshadowed by a crucifix. Jesus said: **"My people, you have people in high places who have given themselves over to the power of the devil. You would recognize these leaders in your government, but they do not tell you who runs their lives. You need to follow their actions and the fruit of their work to know how evil they are. You are dealing with principalities and powers beyond your capability of fighting. That is why you need prayer, My help and your angels to fight this battle of good over evil. With My help you will be able to protect your souls and I will guide you where to go."**

I could see a doctor loading vials of vaccines into a syringe. Jesus said: **"My people, evil men are deceiving the people by placing viruses in shots intended for children and the servicemen. This technique of spreading disease is a goal of the New World Order to limit population growth. As these evil deeds are being uncovered, you need to investigate the source of all vaccines given to the public."**

I could see a fog with a light shining out from a lighthouse. Jesus said: **"My people, be aware of the misleading information given in your news reports. Much of the truth is censored in your news to protect the One World agents. Their identities and their evil meetings of control are kept from the public's eyes. That is why your lives will be endangered if you know too much about their deeds behind the scenes. It is the control of your media and your court system that allows these One World murderers to accomplish their evil deeds. They remove evidence and kill witnesses to allow their people to escape conviction of their crimes. Pray for My help, since one day these evil men will be brought to My justice."**

I could see some new stealth weapons being developed by our military. Jesus said: **"My people, many of your new weapons are being stored for the use of the Antichrist's forces. They will try to use these weapons on My faithful, but I will stop their activ-**

ity and their weapons will be confused not to work. Evil's power is so feeble before My power. When I will give you My protection, Satan and his demons will have no power over you. I will go before you and fight your battles. These proud evil people will be humbled in My sight."

I could see a bright angel marking the faithful. Jesus said: "My people, the evil ones will try to send spies among your prayer groups and meetings. The cross on your foreheads will only be present on My faithful. So, check all of the foreheads of your number to find the spies who do not have this cross. This is another gift I will give you to avoid being captured."

I could see servicemen and police with bright lights directing traffic at night. Jesus said: "My people, I want to forewarn your police and servicemen not to work with your UN leaders. A time will come when certain UN people will try to take away the guns of your police and servicemen. The UN people will then imprison your last arm of protection. As this comes about, your police and servicemen need to go into hiding or they will be killed as any others without the Mark of the Beast. This is a warning I am showing these police and servicemen for their own protection. The Antichrist will try to remove all of your guns and infrastructure of protection."

I could see some massive volcanic eruptions, fires and earthquakes. Jesus said: "My people, I am showing you how I will use natural disasters to confuse the One World people in their attempt to control the world. I will confuse their operations so much, that it will allow many of My faithful to escape to find refuge away from their captors. Rejoice, because I am working miracles against these evil people, just as I defeated the Egyptian soldiers. My angels will help you to fight the demons and evil ones at the Battle of Armageddon. My victory is not far off, so keep faith and trust in your victor. These evil ones will then be cast into Hell and you will enjoy My Era of Peace."

### Friday, August 14, 1998:

After Communion, I could see a large wake of a ship as it turned left. Jesus said: "My people, your ship of state, representing America, has changed its course away from Me. Your choice for president has led you to a position favoring abortion and the fruits of lies and misdeeds. The morals of your government have deteriorated right from the helm. Because you are ignoring the aborted babies and your people care not about sins of the flesh, your justice will demand a loss of your possessions and your freedoms. Natural disasters will be your bed fellows and you are headed for a police state controlled by the United Nations and the New World Order. Your blessings are being stripped, because you have failed to recognize your sins and seek forgiveness. What befalls your country is a consequence of your evil decisions. Until prayer changes your course of action, you are headed for the same end as the Titanic disaster."

Later, at the Benedictine Sisters, Regina Pacie Convent in Bedford, New Hampshire I could see some stone cliffs and a little shop at the bottom of the cliffs. Then across from this scene I saw a beautiful blue spring of water. Jesus said: **"My people, I am showing you a typical refuge that I will provide next to a cave with a spring of blue water. These waters will have healing properties, as I will provide for your food and shelter. I am trying to remove your fear of this time of the Tribulation. There will be some martyred for the Faith, but I will protect many of My faithful from the evil ones. I call you to a faith in My Words that I will provide for you in miraculous ways, so you will know it is from Me alone. My love and peace will stretch out to you to quell all of your fears. Once you are brought to a refuge, no evil will befall you. Your place of protection will be a little harsh, based on your current affluent living, but My Presence will settle your soul and you will be thankful for My protection. This trial will be shortened and you will soon experience a Heaven on earth, when you come to My Era of Peace. This age of My victory will provide you a full opportunity to live in My Divine Will without any presence of evil. Be patient for a while and you will be able to share My Spiritual Presence for as long as you desire each day."**

**Saturday, August 15, 1998:** (Mary's Assumption)

At St. Marie's Church, Manchester, New Hampshire, after Communion, I could see Our Lady of Fatima Statue and then a vision of Mary as at Medjugorje. Finally, I saw her with the light shining around her and she was wearing a crown. Mary said: **"My dear children, this is a sharing of my resurrection into Heaven. It is my sharing completely with my Son's Heart and mine that brought me to Heaven. For I lived only to follow His Will and give example by my life for you to follow as well. I am never without my Son and I lead you to Jesus in all that I do. That is why I encourage all of my children to stay close to my Son in the sacraments, so you can follow His Will in all that He asks of you. In me you can see how to serve my Jesus, for I give all of my being to His service. Do not worry about foolish pride, but take all self out of your life and replace it with Jesus. You were created in His image and He calls each of you to serve Him. Our hearts are so joined together that we live as one. When you are drawn up to Heaven on your resurrection, you will be one with my Son as well."**

Later, at the Little Sisters of St. Francis Adoration, Danville, New Hampshire, I could see an aisle in a chapel and many people came forward carrying banners to the gods of the earth. Jesus said: **"My people, you are looking at the people who follow the gods of the New Age. They are like the pagans of old who worship My creations as gods. They worship the sun, the moon, the earth, and many gods of the earth. This will be the One World religion being proposed by those following the New Age Movement. They are preparing the way for the Antichrist, as they will worship him as a god. This false christ will show great power and wonders and many will be attracted to follow him. All those who believe in Me are a threat to their religion and they will try to kill you for My Name's sake. I will protect My people so that they will not be tested beyond their endurance. This evil lot, who follow the Antichrist, will see their former leaders killed and the Antichrist will assume full power and control over the world. He will rise to this position and think he has conquered Me. It is at the height of his power that I will then dash him and his followers into Hell. I will claim My Triumph and no one will dare to dispute My Kingship. It is after I cleanse the earth of all evil, that I will re-create the earth as it was at the time of Adam. All of My faithful will then live long lives in My**

Era of Peace. Rejoice when My Triumph will strike down the last evil reign of power on the earth."

**Sunday, August 16, 1998:**
At the Little Sisters of St. Francis Adoration, Danville, New Hampshire, I could see a porch to a house and daylight coming to a close. Jesus said: **"My people, you are looking at the coming of the twilight of this age. Since Adam's sin, the world of men and women have taken on a weakness to sin where evil has influenced your lives. Yet, it is a beautiful time of grace. For those who choose to love Me even in the midst of temptation, you are more to be rewarded for facing this test. It is easier to love Me when you are not challenged. But when I test you with difficulties of a job or rude people, will you still love Me? This is the test you must pass in this life, to come to Me in love of your own free will. For you are steeped in your sins, but I have redeemed you. Come to Me for forgiveness and serve Me in My Will and you will find your crown of salvation. This age will soon be tested by an evil whose extent you have yet to see. I am preparing all of My faithful for this time of apostasy with the Antichrist. You will need My help and that of your guardian angel, but do not be fearful. I will give you sufficient graces to endure this trial. Just have faith and trust in Me that I will protect you. Seek Me in every way both in fighting the demons and providing for your food and water. As you are faithful in good times, I ask you to struggle to be faithful even in this Tribulation. Your test will be brief, so just hang on to Me in love and your reward in the splendor of My kingdom will be assured."**

Later, at Mary, Mother of the Church, Newton, New Hampshire, I could see some nuns in three different groups. Then St. Therese visited me and she said: **"My dear children, I want to give encouragement to all of the orders of nuns that you have visited. They are following Jesus' command to love Him and serve Him. It is through His grace that they remain faithful to Him in all of their service and devotion. Jesus sees their good works and He wants them to continue the dedication to the vows they have taken. They affect many lives with their prayers and good works and they inspire many to love Jesus. It is im-**

portant for them to be examples to others of the love that Jesus calls all of you to have for Him and your neighbors. All of the laity are called as well by Jesus to love Him and do good works for others. It is important to sit down and take time to evaluate how you spend your time. Are you spending enough time in prayer, especially in front of the Blessed Sacrament when you can? Are you fasting when possible to restrain your bodily desires? Are you frequenting the sacraments as often as you should? You can call on all of us heavenly intercessors to help you in your work to save souls. We are ever ready to encourage your work for the Lord. Give daily thanks to Jesus for every opportunity to praise Him and bring souls to Him."

### Monday, August 17, 1998:

After Communion, I could see a large drain. Jesus said: "My people, as Ezechiel has foretold Israel's fall, so I am telling you now, that America is about to fall as well. All of your freedoms and all of your wealth will be brought low. Just as Israel was taken over by its enemies, you too will have another tyrant controlling your nation. People will be upset with this prophecy, as the people of Israel were upset with My prophets. I tell you, the time of your falling into ruin is not far off. Prepare, My people, for the New World Order is about to come to power. You will be tested as never before with destruction and persecution. Seek My help and I will protect your souls. Many will have to suffer and some even martyrdom, but evil will have its day. I will then bring this evil lot to its ruination with one swift blow of My might. Then all of these evil people will be brought to My justice and they will be cast into the eternal flames of Hell. My faithful will then enjoy My Era of Peace with no evil in My sight."

### Tuesday, August 18, 1998:

At St. Mary Queen of Creation Church, New Baltimore, Michigan, after Communion, I could see a rich gold altar. Jesus said: "My people, I have told you many times before that it is what is in your heart that matters. Do you grow rich for yourself or for My intentions? There are many proper needs for money in your houses, your transportation, and the education of your children. Your intentions need to be noble in sharing your money both in charities and for your family's welfare. It is really about excesses that you should be concerned. To have enough for one's needs is proper, but to store huge piles of wealth, just to be rich for yourself, is approaching a sin of avarice. Do not desire money for its own sake, since I told you that you can only have one master. You are either going to love the world and its riches or you will love Me. You cannot love both. Consider yourself as a good steward of the goods that I have given you. You are here for a short time and you are given to manage your own affairs. When you come to the judgment, you will have to make an accounting of your actions. I will look into the heart for your intentions. If you dealt fairly with your neighbor and shared your possessions, I will welcome you into an eternal rich life in Heaven. But if you were selfish with your spending and you did not help your neighbor, you will have to account for your greed. A rich man can be saved, but He must be willing to give everything up and follow My Will."

**Wednesday, August 19, 1998:**

At St. Mary, Queen of Creation Church, New Baltimore, Michigan, after Communion, I could see Jesus standing and leading people in the darkness of a church. Jesus said: **"My people, I am the Good Shepherd and My sheep follow My voice. My bishops need your prayers dearly, especially in this age of apostasy. There are many evil forces in the world working for control over My Church. Pray that these bishops will not succumb to the ways of the world or selfish pride. Some of My sheep are being misled by some wayward bishops. Pride in power and prestige can lead even bishops into false ways. Pray, My children, to follow My voice and discern the proper faith to follow. When someone deviates from the teachings of the Gospel, do not follow them and only follow Me. There are some bishops that are not following Me that are in deep need of your prayers. The flesh is weak even among My bishops, but those, who mislead My faithful, will have to answer to My justice. I love you, My children, and I am always watching out for your** protection. Come, follow Me as I carry My sheep into My Era of Peace. I will lead you safely, even through the darkness of the Tribulation."

Later, at St. Lucy's Adoration, Troy, Michigan, I could see many cars on busy intersections. Jesus said: "My people, many times you are always in a rush through life. Your fast paced living needs to be slowed down because you need to analyze your intentions more. Do not let the little annoyances in life make you impatient or angry with others. When you are driving on the road in your car, you need to be more patient with other drivers. Time is not that important, if you are going to be venting your anger at every slow down in traffic. You need to calm yourself and think of each of these opportunities as a test of your patience. If you practice charity and you are intent on pleasing Me, then you will be able to weather each storm. If you let your temper run your life, then you will be facing one difficulty after another. Your whole lifetime is a test to prove how much you love Me and how you can serve Me lovingly. I did not make you to live a fast life. Take each challenge in faith and be resolute in not losing your temper over the little things in life."

**Thursday, August 20, 1998:** (St. Bernard)

After Communion, I could see the inside of a church and there was a large chute where dirt and dark brown debris were flowing into the church. Jesus said: "My people, there are many ways that the filth of sin and apostasy are flowing into My Church. Both some priests and lay teachers are bringing in false teachings to mislead My faithful. The teachings on the marriage act and sins of the flesh are being misrepresented and the serious nature of sin is not being emphasized. Serious problems in your society, concerning life styles affecting the family, are not being properly addressed or taught. Even the Sacrament of Reconciliation is not being promoted or it is being ignored. All of this filth of bad teaching is an evil attempt to snuff out the life of My Church. This will culminate in a schism in My Church when many will refuse to follow My Laws put forward through Pope John Paul II's teachings. So, I ask My faithful to pray for discernment and to not be afraid to speak out when error is being promoted, even by priests."

Later, at the prayer group, I saw a garage and it slowly crumbled from an explosion. Jesus said: "My people of America, you may feel justified in self-defense as an excuse for your actions. But continuing a cycle of killing and destruction is the work of the evil one. Pray for peace, My children, or your fighting may consume you in a greater war. Those who kill in planned events will have to answer for these lives at the judgment."

I could see several houses with people looking out of their windows. Jesus said: "My people, as terrorists increase their destruction, fear of counterattacks will cause you to be in armed camps, fearful to carry on your lives. Those evil killers will answer to My justice, but do not use this as an excuse to create a police state under martial law. There is a more devious plan behind all of this activity where only the One World people know the answer. Do not react to evil with a worse evil."

I could see some special warheads being loaded on missiles underground next to the dirt. Jesus said: "My people, the repercussions of your current actions will enrage plans for a further escalation of a potential war. You will see a cycle of evil feelings between various countries who will become polarized in different camps. Unless this rampant destruction ceases, ever worse retaliations will occur. The evil one is intent on destroying all of mankind, so do not help him by spreading more serious actions."

I could see the Holy Father holding his staff and his feet were above a sloping hill of houses. Jesus said: "My people, you are seeing how My Pope son John Paul II is slowly slipping in his control of the Churches. His health and his control over the Church are heading downhill. Events will move quickly after the warning, as many of his cardinals will try to remove him from office. When he does leave Rome, your schism will begin. Pray for the Holy Father."

I could see many large cisterns of water being destroyed. Jesus said: "My people, I have warned you to save some food for the time before the Tribulation. This food will be scarce and very controlled by the One World people. As you were witness to the broken water main, water will be controlled as well by the One World people. So save plenty of water for your needs as well. In all of this, have no fear, for I will multiply what you have and I will provide for your needs."

I could see some wooden barns with various rooms. Jesus said: "My people, I am showing you how many people have been warned to store food in refuge places. The food you will save is not to be hoarded, but shared with all of those who come to the refuges. You will see Me multiply food at many refuge sites. Have trust in My help and pray for courage in your spiritual battle against the evil ones."

I could see many empty store shelves as a famine spread over the land. Jesus said: "My people, you must realize how dangerous your riots will become when people are hungry and desperate. What little food that is left, some will fight over. Give your food out while it is calm, but as terror spreads in fighting for food, this is the time to leave your homes in haste. Whatever food you take with you, I will continue to multiply for you. Have total faith in My help and you will see how I will provide for all of your needs."

**Friday, August 21, 1998:**

After Communion, I could see a deep hole in the ground with money and decayed bones at the bottom. Jesus said: **"My people, I am showing you this old grave because your life is very short on earth. You came into this world without anything and you will leave in the same way. There is no reason, therefore, to be in love with anything of a worldly nature, because it will pass away as your body. Do not feel that you would like to stay here, since you were created to be with Me in Heaven. Instead of spending most of your time on worldly things, you should be focused more on your soul's destination. Your soul is immortal and will last forever beyond the grave. Unless you die to self and follow My Will, you cannot come to Heaven. You are here to serve Me, love Me, and serve your neighbor. By following My Commandments to love God and your neighbor as yourself, you will be on a road to be resurrected to Heaven. Think more of where you are going after the grave, since you will be** there forever. If you live for yourself only, you will be forever suffering in Hell. Living for Me will bring you to eternal ecstasy in Heaven. The choice is yours."

(Note: In coming to Adoration I saw what could have been a meteor or some fireworks on the side of the road. There was a white light that came out of the sky and just disappeared.) At Adoration, I could see in vision a bright light from a comet as it came on a curved orbit right toward the earth. As it circled the earth I saw many orange plumes of fire spread out in all directions. Jesus said: **"My people, I am showing you again the comet of My great chastisement that will be My triumph over Satan. This comet is already on its way to your planet, but the scientists are not revealing it. As it starts to approach you, many will see it and it will no longer be a secret. The missiles that will be sent to destroy it will not work as My angels will deter them. What is meant to happen will not be changed by mankind. There will be great flames that will burn those who are not faithful. These will suffer a Hell on earth before they are cast into Hell. My will is to be accomplished in My time and by My design. Those who are faithful will be protected from these flames of My justice. Evil will be cleansed from the earth and My faithful will live in My Era of Peace in a paradise on earth. Have courage to endure this Tribulation and you will be rewarded."**

**Saturday, August 22, 1998:** (Queenship of Mary)

After Communion, I could see a statue of Mary and then Mary in a wedding gown. Mary said: **"My dear children, Jesus has gifted me with a virgin birth. He has raised me up to Heaven and I have been crowned Queen of Heaven. Just as my Son has been so gracious to me, He will give all of you the treasure of Heaven, if you follow His Will. To serve Jesus you must have a burning desire to love Him from your heart. He is the Spouse of His Church and He has an infinite love for each individual soul. You are all special in His eyes and He calls each of you to say 'yes' to Him. You are all called to have proper white garments on, ready to go to meet the Bridegroom. By frequent Confession, you will always be ready to enter the wedding feast in Heaven."**

Later, after Communion, I could see Jean Marie and Al Bello at their wedding and there were angels standing around them. Jesus said: **"My dear children, a wedding is a uniting of two lives as I am united to My Church. Each life is committed in love and faith to each other and I am in their midst through My Sacramental Presence. Love is the binding force that holds couples and societies together. It is love between man and wife that mirrors My love for My faithful. Everything you do should be done out of love, if it is to have any meaning. Even at Cana, I took compassion on the couple at My mother's invitation. I let you provide for yourselves and then with My help I bring you a much finer wine. Those that fail on their own attempts need to follow My Will and everything will be provided for you. Live on in My love and you will not be far from enjoying My Kingdom in Heaven."**

### Sunday, August 23, 1998:

After Communion, I could see a dividing line where those on one side were against God and those faithful on the other side. There were also several attacks of an evil wolf eye. Jesus said: **"My people, I have allowed the good to live among the bad, giving each an equal opportunity to be saved. At the judgment I will separate the wheat from the tares. You are seeing this separation, because there will be a sifting of lives based on how they lived on the earth. Those who followed My Commandments and cared for Me and their neighbors will be gathered into My barn. Those who were selfish and obeyed only their own will will be cast into the fire to be burned forever in Hell. The narrow road is when you follow My Will and not your own. This is the path of love that I call all of My faithful to follow. You will see demons come in various forms and distractions to try and detour you from following Me. Seek My help in My Sacraments and you will be strengthened to stay the course and win the battle against evil in saving your soul. I did not say it would be easy. You will have to struggle in pain during life, but your struggle will be worth your heavenly reward."**

Later, at Adoration, I could see a circling storm as a hurricane causing much damage. Jesus said: **"My people, I have told you** that you will be tested by storms and fires. Many have been killed this year already from tornadoes. After this year passes, it will be marked by how much damage has been done. You are concerned about terrorists, but you will see that natural disasters will cause you more grief. Many have been already brought to their knees because of the storms and fires. These events will continue with many disasters in succession. My blessings have protected you from disasters in years gone by, but your sins will haunt you when I withdraw My arm of protection. You will see continuing chastisements for all of your many sins against Me of abortion and sins of the flesh. You will repeat the history of Israel's disasters which occurred when they refused to follow My ways. Wake up, America, and get on your knees in prayer or you will endure further punishment for your sins. If you fail to listen to My Words, your fall will be imminent."

**Monday, August 24, 1998:**
After Communion, I could see a large spider web and a symbol of the United Nations was in the middle. Jesus said: "**My people, many things in your world are not apparent because there is an invisible force behind all that happens. All that happens on a human world scale is very controlled by the One World People of money and power. This is represented by an invisible spider web which can only be seen and recognized with a proper light. The World Bank, the International Monetary Fund and the United Nations are but a few of the organizations under the control of the One World people. Many of the national banks and stock markets are under their control as well. These preparations for a world takeover by the so called New World Order are all orchestrated to allow the Antichrist a base to control the world. These forces have been working quietly to control the world's money, food, communications, and even some governments. Despite all of the evil one's influence on world events, I will still be victorious because My power is supreme. I will dispatch My angels to gather up all the grapes at the harvest of souls and all of these evil powers will be vanquished. So, have no fear of the many secret bases of power who think they hold control over the world. Their reign is brief and futile against my justice.**"

Later, at Adoration, I could look down on a large, long wedding banquet. I could see all of the chairs were specially placed with names on them. Jesus said: "**My people, I am giving you a glimpse of the wedding feast that I am calling all of My faithful to come and enjoy. All of the places have been set by name, because I told you that I am going to prepare a place for you. You will share in My peace and love forever. This feast represents My love for My Church as in a marriage. Because you have been faithful to Me, I will keep My promise of presenting you before My Father. How could you refuse to come to My wedding feast when all of you are invited? If everyone would take time to realize how glorious Heaven is, there would be no other obvious choice. It is only because some refuse My love, that these poor souls will miss their eternal calling. Teach all of those you can reach of My love and share My promise of eternal happiness in Heaven. The angels praise Me continuously as they appreciate the gift of My glory in Heaven. So come, share My heavenly feast by loving Me and doing My Will."**

**Tuesday, August 25, 1998:**

After Communion, I could see two separate arches that represented two Churches. Jesus said: "**My people, I am preparing you for the coming schism in the Church that will split My Church in two. My remnant will have to have their Masses underground in their homes. In addition to Mass needs, it will be necessary that you are versed well in your faith. Many false theologians will come forward saying how great the Antipope is. By knowing the faith given by the Apostles, you will be able to refute new heresies and blasphemies that will be used to mislead My faithful. You will be given the grace and courage to break away from this new false church that will claim its roots in Me. As true doctrines will be denied and new false dogmas will be proclaimed, people will be forced to chose between My Remnant and the Antipope. This is why you will need your old Bibles and your Catechisms to show the tenets of My true Faith and the deceptions of the evil ones. By standing firm in your beliefs, you will save your souls."**

Later, at Adoration, I could see tornadoes and major storms with a lot of rain and wind. Jesus said: **"My people, brace yourselves, for you are about to be pummeled by many serious storms. The intensity of events will increase as well as the extent of damage. You will clean up from one storm only to make ready for the next one. When you see how awesome the power of nature is, there will be no doubt that these are chastisements from My hand. As many are stripped of their possessions, your economy will start to reel from these events. All of man's plans will be dashed to pieces. As these events accumulate, you will beg for My mercy. Until you are brought low and your affluence humbled, you will not desire to follow My Will. When you see how futile your attempts are before My wrath, you will come to your knees in prayer. Those who defy My authority and will not follow My Will will pay dearly for their disbelief. Prayer is your only weapon to lessen these chastisements. It is your sin and your stubbornness to seek My forgiveness that is calling down these storms."**

**Wednesday, August 26, 1998:**
After Communion, I could see some tall columns of clouds as in multiple tornadoes. Jesus said: **"My people, as you reprimand your children, I am reprimanding My children as well through your weather. It is not My desire to bring My justice upon you, but it is your sins that are calling for your retribution. Still others do not always link your hardships to your sins. I have told you before to read the signs of your times as the violence of your killing is reflected in the violence of your storms. Your sins are exacting a punishment that your nation is paying dearly. As your sins of violence continue, you can expect similar events to continue. Pray that your people will understand their erring ways and they will get on their knees in prayer."**

**Thursday, August 27, 1998:** (St. Monica)
After Communion, I could see a stone wall and someone struggling to find their way. Jesus said: **"My people, many times in life you come up against barriers that appear to have no way around**

them. When you are faced with such problems, do not give up. If your struggle is worthwhile, ask for the impossible in prayer and if it is in My Will, you may find a way around your problem. At other times, if your problem is a person's stubbornness, that soul may be changed by an openness to prayer. Persistence in prayer may be required when there is a high price on the soul involved. So, take courage in all of life's struggles. You may not be successful at first, but by your persistence, you may resolve many physical and spiritual problems. Always seek My help in a desperate moment and I will hear your prayer. Focus your attention on things for the well-being of your soul and that of other souls. These areas are more fertile ground to have prayer answered. Remember that nothing is impossible with Me. A person who is humble and consistent in their prayer will have a better hearing before Me."

Later, at the prayer group, I could see some gold things and jewelry at a carnival stand. Jesus said: "My people, do not crave or worship your valuables as a god in your life. The beauty of jewelry and gold objects attracts the eye. Do not flaunt these possessions as showing off in pride how rich you are. These earthly treasures count for nothing in Heaven. Seek to accumulate heavenly treasures by your good deeds, rather than becoming rich for yourself. Just as some are attracted to imitation valuables, do not be taken in by the world's attraction to possessions."

I could see a striped animal. Jesus said: "My people, many animals do not change their stripes or their spots. This is true of mankind in many ways. Even though you would like to change people's ways, it is not easy to change bad habits. It is only by My grace and prayer that people can be converted. In the last analysis, that person has to desire a change in their life. Keep praying and giving good example for those not following My ways. Some may change with persistent prayer, but it is difficult to change human nature."

I could see some bombs and a fire in the background. Jesus said: "My people, terrorism relies on surprise and massive devastation to push their political goals. This is a cowardly deed, no matter how much these terrorists claim to be motivated. **Killing innocent lives indiscriminately is a violation of My law and can never be justified. All those who participate in these deeds will have to answer for each life lost at the judgment. You would be surprised to see who is really behind these deadly acts.**"

I could see some missiles being launched and many fires came as they struck their targets. Jesus said: "**My people, take care that you do not incite further destruction by any of your reprisals. I have told you that each destructive act will cause enough anger and hatred to initiate even worse destruction. Control your responses or a major war could break out. Pray for peace and compromise or your weapons will be used.**"

I could see charts of hurricane frequencies and the mild response of those affected in a recent storm. Jesus said: "**My people, do not flaunt My chastisements as nothing. You may see succeeding storms tear down your arrogant attitude. Just as you may be relieved for now, do not think that your testing is over. More storms are coming until you will be tired of Nature humbling your possessions. Pray for mitigating these storms, instead of dismissing them as nothing.**"

I could see some flooding between some large hills. Jesus said: "**My people, I have told you to move to higher ground and back from rivers and oceans. Many of your floods this year have come in these areas. Heed My Words, since you will continue to see many such disasters. Seek the safety of high ground both on earth and in spiritual things. By going to safe havens in the test of the Tribulation, you will be protected from the evil men and evil spirits. Those who fail to heed My Words will be swept away by the water or by the power of the Antichrist.**"

I could see some men in black uniforms planning an attack. Later, flames came from a building. Jesus said: "**My people, evil men are planning many of these explosions that are claimed to be caused by some political factions. In actuality, many are financed by the One World people that are behind these deeds. By destroying governments and creating chaos, the agents of the Antichrist are laying the roots for their world takeover. The evil ones are behind many of these terrible crimes of mass killings. You will be tested by evil, but My power will be victo-**

rious. Have hope and faith in My protection and your souls will be saved. Satan will have no power over My faithful in My safe havens."

Friday, August 28, 1998:

At Fernandez's House, Corpus Christi, Texas, by a statue in the yard, I could smell roses and Our Lady appeared in a crown. Mary said: "**My dear children, your test of the spirit in this statue lies in the hearts of those who come here to pray. Any little miracles received are little touches to strengthen my children's faith. Do not look for miracles, but look for the devotion I bring people to say my Rosary. As I bring souls to pray, I lead them to my Son, Jesus as well. Keep focused on our Two Hearts in prayer and your requests will be cared for. Believe that my love reaches out to all those that give devotion to me. This statue is a public witness to bring souls to prayer.**"

Later, at Most Precious Blood Church at Corpus Christi, Texas, after Communion, I could see a military person as in the Russian Army and behind him was a dark closed church. Jesus said: "**My people, I call your attention to how easily a government can meet its demise as in Russia. From day one the Communist government has been influenced by the men of money. This is a country that was strongly Catholic at one time. Yet, it became a puppet for communism and atheism. All religions were persecuted and the people had to worship in secret. Because they killed the priests and have held up man as their god, this country is on the brink of ruin. Let this be a lesson to you in America, how quickly you can lose everything when you turn your back on Me. You are being ruled by a madness over the separation of Church and state. In order to give a freedom to worship, you are advocating no religion in its place. The resultant atheism is no different than in Russia, because you monetarily punish those using any public monies for religious purposes. Your economy may seem strong today, but you could be like Russia tomorrow facing ruin. Take notice, America, if you continue to deny Me as a country by your sins of abortion and your persecution of the religious, you too, will suffer ruination. Your government can be toppled by these same men of money, and at** the proper time you will be given over to the power of the Antichrist. Pray, My people, for My help in protecting your souls and I will defy all evil power on earth. Trust in Me and your soul will be saved."

**Saturday, August 29, 1998:** (Martyrdom of St. John the Baptist) At the Most Precious Blood Church, Corpus Christi, Texas, after Communion, I could see six women dressed in black for someone that was killed. Jesus said: **"My people, I draw your attention to all of the killing going on in your world. You think how barbaric the killing of St. John the Baptist was, but your society also has such little regard for life. If you think that you are more civilized today, then how do you explain the slaughter of your innocent babies? Each life is precious, no matter what your people reason about the value of certain lives. It is this death mentality that you need to pray for your people to change. It is bad enough to kill out of hatred or vengeance, but it is even worse to see people killed or infants with no feeling in the hearts of these killers. All killing is abhorrent because it denies My plan for these lives. For each killing, I will hold these souls accountable at their judgment. Pray to stop abortions and pray for peace in your world. The anger between nations is so strained, that violence and war is very commonplace in your world. Pray also that your TV should not be showing your children this violent programming. Your people need to share love and neighborly help to change all of the evil hatred inflicted by Satan. Counter all of the evil you see with love and good example. Each life can bring a good influence to fight all of the evil in your world. A day is coming when I will cleanse all evil from the earth. Be ready, My children, by frequent Confession, so your souls will be acceptable in My sight."**

Later, at St. Philip the Apostle Church, Corpus Christi, Texas, I could see someone standing and there was a spinning universe behind that person. Jesus said: **"My people, do not think that the world centers around your life. Instead of looking for others to serve you, you must serve your neighbor. If you are to be great in the eyes of Heaven, then you must serve everyone, as I told My Apostles. It is a humble and contrite heart that I value most** before other souls. Do not think you are great, if you are a success in the world. Give credit to Me for all that you have and for all that you have accomplished. In your prayers after Communion give thanks to Me for all of the gifts I have given you to accomplish your good deeds. I have asked you to come to Me in the innocence of a little child to let Me guide you in following My Will. By giving over your will to Me, I can mold you into the person you are in building up My Kingdom. Look to be more successful in the eyes of Heaven rather than the success of the world."

### Sunday, August 30, 1998:

At St. Philip the Apostle, Corpus Christi, Texas, after Communion, I could see some people sitting and standing in the back of church. Jesus said: "My people, all of you are most precious in My sight. You are all creations of My Will and you are beautiful because you came from My hand. In the world's eyes beauty is only skin deep, but I look into the inner beauty of each soul. Just as I chastised the Pharisees, be attentive to your inner beauty of the soul as with your outer appearances. At Baptism your soul is white and gleaming, but as sin enters in, you can become hideous to Me. So renew your soul's beauty by frequent Confession. When you come to Me in sorrow for your sins, I will forgive you and make you radiant again in My sight. No matter what your outer appearances may seem to the world, always show joy in your face and share the beauty and love that you have within. Do not be depressed, but raise your spirits to show Me that you are happy to be alive in serving Me. The more you share your love and concern for your neighbor, the more you can lift their spirits toward peace in your world. When you seek the joy of being with Me in Heaven, you will be better able to suffer all of life's little difficulties."

### Monday, August 31, 1998:

At St. Mary's Church, San Antonio, Texas, after Communion, I could see an altar in church and the scene drifted from the foot of the altar up slowly to view the Host in a monstrance. Jesus said: "My people, come to visit Me in My Blessed Sacrament so you can give Me praise and glory. If you could only view all of My angels and the cohort of saints, you could see how they praise Me at all times in humble homage. I am your King, your Creator, and also your Redeemer. I have loved all of My children so much that I gave up My life for your sins, so you could one day come to Heaven. You do not realize the unending joy that awaits all who are faithful to My Will. People ask what will I do in Heaven? Will I be bored? I tell you, My children, these are only earthly thoughts. When you are in My beatific vision, you will see and experience an infinite love and peace and you will ask no more questions. You will be in such awe of My magnificence, your soul will stand before the truth of your existence and bow down in worship. I am the Life and the Resurrection. Your soul has only one desire and that is to be with Me forever. Nothing will give your soul peace and rest, except My Presence. So rejoice in My Real Presence in My Host, for you are experiencing there a small taste of Heaven. Come and do My Will and your soul will be granted eternal rest with Me in Heaven."

Later, at Adoration, I could see a wooden pier going out into a muddy brown river. Jesus said: "My people, great dark clouds are on America's horizon. You are being tested with damage from storms, droughts, and now the unsettled economies around the world. The result is the same in that you will be stripped of your possessions. Both the financial markets and the destruction of the storms are adding up some huge losses. Even though you claim to have a good economy, you still are very vulnerable. Many of these markets and terrorism can be manipulated, but these things have many countries uncertain of their futures. It is this kind of chaotic condition that will eventually lead to the Antichrist's takeover. You are seeing the early warning signs for his preparation. Many of your world leaders are in difficult times and they will be forced out of their offices over time. Pray for spiritual strength to endure this coming Tribulation."

**Tuesday, September 1, 1998:**

After Communion, I could see a shining floor with a broken picture face down. Jesus said: "My people, when a picture falls off the wall or when a person you know moves away, the memory of that person becomes difficult over time. Each person in your life is a gift for a short time and a brief opportunity to know that person. Think of how each person has affected your life. Then you can imagine how you affect the lives you encounter. You are only here a short time, so take advantage of that time to be a holy influence on those you meet. Those people that you really love, you would find a reason and a way to have their pictures restored on your walls. So keep My picture and that of the saints in your churches and homes, so you can remember Me always and the ones you love the most."

Later, at Adoration, I could see some green spores and a sticky substance representing germ warfare of bacteria and viruses. Jesus said: "My people, there will be attempts by your military to start spreading germ warfare in various parts of your country as experiments. As the time of the Tribulation draws near, these evil men will be spreading disease germs in rural areas where they suspect My faithful of hiding. You will be protected by My angels at all of My safe havens and the caves from any sickness. Look on the white luminous crosses or drink the healing waters at the caves and you will be healed of any plagues or diseases. You will be safe at these places from any weapons or detection equipment. Have trust in My help to protect your bodies and your souls from evil men and the demons. Pray for My help at all times and your souls will be saved."

**Wednesday, September 2, 1998:**

After Communion, I could see someone standing between two mirrors where you could see multiple reflections. Jesus said: "My people, before you criticize others, take a look at your own actions. Look in the mirror and think how you appear before those around you. Do you have a sour look of constant anger displays? Are you always complaining of people's actions or your daily difficulties? Are you gossiping about others either truthfully or wrongfully? Remember that your actions speak louder than your words. You have My sacraments of grace among you, so you should be filled with joy and faith in being safe with Me. Always be joyful and smiling even among your problems, because you need to lift the spirits of your neighbors. Do not be complaining or gossiping, but by your encouragement and holy life, give good example to others. Show love to each person whether you like them or not. If people could convict you of being a Christian by your actions, then you are doing only your duty. Imitate My life in all I did for people and you will have a model and a goal for your life. By having a positive attitude through the Holy Spirit, you will spread the Faith among the nations. Always be conscious of how you appear before others and teach them by your good example."

**Thursday, September 3, 1998:**
After Communion, I could see a large flame in a mirror. Jesus said: "**My people, I am showing you the cleansing fire of My purification. You are being tested with fires in your physical world or suffering in other ways. All that you are suffering on the earth can be applied to the temporal punishment due for your sins. So do not waste your pain on earth that can be used to spare some time in Purgatory. All of your stripping of your possessions is better for your soul, since your accumulated wealth makes you feel more dependent on your means, instead of Me. This cleansing fire of My purification is meant to ready you for coming to Heaven. Until you have reached a state of perfection in living My Divine Will, you are not ready to enter Heaven. Only those souls with white garments of perfection are allowed entry into Heaven. All souls by their free will have to accept Me as Savior and give Me praise each day. Many souls require time in Purgatory to reach this state of perfection after suffering the flames of My justice. The less sins you commit and the more suffering you offer up, will lessen your time in Purgatory. So strive each day to get closer to following My Will and you will draw closer to the day of being with Me in Heaven. I created you to be with Me in Heaven. Now you must struggle in every way possible to reach for your place in My glory.**"

Later, at the prayer group, I could see a ship's bow as it cut through the water. A light shown on the ship for a while and then it traveled off into the dark. Jesus said: "**My people, this ship represents America. When it traveled in the light of My grace, you had many blessings as a rich nation. Now, because of your sins** of abortion and your sins of the flesh, you are traveling in the darkness of your sins. I will strip My blessings from the unworthy as you have determined your fate of punishment."

I could see many expensive cars traveling in a funeral procession. Jesus said: "My people of America, this march is to your own funeral. By the abuses of power and your turning your back on Me, you will see your nation lose its rights and freedoms. Evil men will change your country into a tyrannical police state. The One World people of power and money will take their rule in preparation for the Antichrist. You will not see justice on the earth until I come in triumph. With My coming on the clouds, I will strike down all evil and remove it from the earth. Have hope in My victory which is coming soon."

I could see many tanks and a picture of a red star in Russia. Jesus said: "My people, communism will return to Russia because it never left. The evil men who gave a sign of peace and capitalism were only acting out a plan of the One World people who sponsored communism from the beginning. There will be dictatorial power threatening world stability once again. Russia will also be made ready for the Antichrist to assume power."

I could see a woman dressed in robes as in older days. Jesus said: "My people, those associated with communistic principles have tried to make men and women equal so their labor can be abused. The families have been ruined by the work of the extreme feminists. By forcing women into the work force, for even an existence in some families, you have laid the groundwork for your nation's demise. Divorce and exploitation of women are now the results of these so called freedoms. The children are now the victims of a day care mentality that has left motherly love on the sideline. See that all the riches in the world will not replace the love between a mother and child."

I could see a hill with seven lamp stands ascending to the top. Jesus said: "My people, these are the great economic nations in the world, but they are about to fall from their thrones. Look around you, My people, there are many signs of a world economic collapse about to happen. But look deeper into who holds the real purse strings in these countries. The Federal Reserve represents only the rich bankers, but they hold all of your powers of finance. This is true in the central banks of other countries as well. These are the men about to bring about the One World order. They will create a collapse to steal everyone's money so they can take control of the world. All of this power will then be laid in front of the Antichrist who will lead chaos back to a seeming peace. Prepare for these events and pray for My protection as you enter the great Tribulation."

I could see crowds of people out of work looking for food and jobs. Jesus said: "My people, history will repeat itself once again as a world depression will come among you. Do not ever take the Mark of the Beast which the agents of the Antichrist will offer for jobs and food. Instead, seek My help and that of your guardian angels to provide for your food and shelter in My safe havens and the caves. By placing full trust in Me, I will provide for all of your needs as I did for My people in the Exodus."

I could see a dark church with a small light on the altar. Jesus said: "My people, the fall of your churches is not far off. Once the Antipope comes to power, he will reign over the churches. The darkness represents the evil ways by which My churches will be undermined. A schism will send My remnant into underground Masses and the Antipope will mislead others to worship the Antichrist. After the Antipope takes power, My faithful will be forced to leave these evil infested churches. Look to My strength for a moment, then I will lay these evil people low as I will bring My victory."

**Friday, September 4, 1998:**

After Communion, I could see a musical symbol in wood on a piano. Jesus said: "My people, music is My gift to you, because all Heaven is abound with the singing of My choirs of angels. You have been graced with the inspiration of many beautiful song writers and composers. Even the Psalms are songs. Singing praises to Me is inspirational and it complements your worship at Mass. I have given you, My son, this vision and sound of My angels singing. So you know how beautiful it is to imitate the angels in giving Me honor and praise. There are other elements in your modern music that Satan has placed in evil hearts. These elements only arouse earthly feelings and many are associated with drugs and satanic influences. **Avoid this side of music which does not bring you closer to Me. Be joyous in heart and share these heavenly songs which lift the spirit and keep you focused on Me.**"

Later, at Adoration, I could see a man sitting at a picnic table in a small house. I then could see several satellites circling the earth. Jesus said: **"My people, you are comfortable now with all of your cars and electrical devices. A time is coming with the Tribulation, that you will have to go into hiding with only a few things on your back. You will be led to either refuges or caves. You will then be living a simple life without all of your conveniences. You will have to depend totally on My help to provide you food and shelter. You will be living a simple and crude existence, but you will see Me defend you from all of the evil men and evil spirits. Your inventions will be no match for My power. The spiritual warfare will be the most important. By asking for My help and that of your guardian angels, I will protect your souls from evil. Keep focused on Me and you will see paradise in the new Era of Peace, which will be more beautiful than your present existence. When you will be living in the Divine Will, you will wonder why you would want any other way to live. By following My Will completely, you will have full knowledge to know and love Me.**"

**Saturday, September 5, 1998:**

After Communion, I could see some tents being set up and a man was peering into the tent. Jesus said: **"My people, in the days in the desert My people reverenced the Holy of Holies which housed the Ark of the Covenant. Moses led the people to keep holy the Sabbath and the Tablets of the Commandments were kept in a reserved place in the tents. But you have a greater than Moses here in My Presence. Today, you have My Body and Blood present in the Host which is stored in your many Tabernacles. That is why I want you to reverence My Real Presence in the Host as My being with you at every moment. By genuflecting and receiving Me without mortal sin on your souls, you are giving Me honor and glory.**"

At St. Louis Church, at Leo and Colleen Sarantino's wedding, I saw a couple getting married and there were several angels watching over them. Jesus said: "**My people, I am showing you in this vision how the guardian angels of all of the couple's future children are assigned to you when you get married. The Sacrament of Marriage is the veil of protection for My people to have children. Children, conceived out of wedlock, are robbed of My graces of My Sacrament of Marriage. You are sharing in My creation as you are the instruments to bring forth new life. I bestow the spirit of life on a new soul at the moment of conception. Just as your children's souls are ready to be united in a body, so their angels wait in eager readiness as well. You are being protected by My angels from birth, so rejoice that Heaven is attentive to each soul's importance. You are all individually unique, meaning that no one will ever have your exact gifts. That is why it is so important not to deny the existence of My children's souls through abortion. Rejoice in the love between married couples, for it is My model for My love for My Church.**"

### Sunday, September 6, 1998:

After Communion, I could see a bishop standing next to a large crucifix. Jesus said: "**My people, everyone is called to carry their cross, even the bishops and cardinals. These men have a duty to spread My Gospel teaching in the way it was passed down from the Apostles. They have a heavy responsibility for the souls under their care. They also will be responsible for any souls who are misled by their false teaching. Pray for your clergy, My people, for their words affect many listening to them. Pray that when the schism comes, your priests and bishops will follow the teachings of My present Pope John Paul II, instead of the Antipope. This is an evil age of apostasy and many souls will be misled by evil influences. It is important, My faithful, to prepare to be strong in your faith, because there will be some to persuade you to follow the Antichrist. Never worship any other person or idols, but Me. Never take a chip in your hand or forehead. Trust in Me to lead you and I will protect your soul and provide for your needs.**"

Later, at Adoration, I could see Mary in heaven and there was a splendid glow of gold color all around her for some distance. Mary said: "**My dear children, I am showing you how my Son** has blessed me with so many gifts. I have come to you in many messages and apparitions in many places all over the world. Many of the faithful have heard these messages, but few are acting on the prayer life that I requested. I came to announce my Son's Second Coming and prepare you for the last of Satan's attempts to steal souls from my Son. Go back and re-read my messages in the light of what is happening today. Everything will be fulfilled that was foretold to you in the Scriptures. Pray much, my children, for you will be tested dearly."

Monday, September 7, 1998: (Labor Day)

After Communion, I could see a fence in the shape of a heart. Jesus said: "My people, I ask each of you to give Me your labor of love by carrying your cross daily. Since Adam and Eve were cast out of the Garden of Eden, mankind has been condemned to work by the sweat of his brow. Working with your hands is the vocation that many of you can use for your salvation. It is by dedicating your lives to My service that you will find your way to Heaven. It is just also that each person should do their fair share in being responsible for themselves. Reach out to help your neighbor when they are unable to help themselves. The fruit of your labor comes in knowing that you have accomplished your duty. You have only a short time on earth, so live it to the fullest in carrying out My plan for your lives."

Later, at Adoration, I could see some armies preparing for war. Jesus said: "My people, why do you let the evil one enrage your anger into a war of killing? Struggle to be at peace and not seeking revenge or taking of another's land. The more you seek to gain, the more futile is your quest. Whatever you gain by cheating or fighting will only whet your appetite for more. Do not let feelings or greed run your life. When you give into your desires without studying the consequences, you may have to deal with affecting the lives of others. You have no right to take another's life for any kind of gain. Pray and seek peace, for peace should be everyone's goal. Many fight over minor religious differences or over very little gains. Refuse to fight battles that place lives in danger. Battling for freedom or self defense may be justified in men's eyes, but to Me the preservation of life is the most precious. Satan hates man and he does everything to get you to fight each other. By keeping love and following My Will as your focus, nothing will come between you and Me. Pray constantly for peace and strive as well to be peacemakers to those around you."

Tuesday, September 8, 1998: (Birth of Mary)
After Communion, I could see a snake striking with its fangs showing and then there was darkness. Jesus said: "**My people, you can see all around in the world how Satan has placed his venom of sin in many hearts. When things are going well and people can afford what they need, they get very complacent and forget their prayers. For many it takes hardships or tough times to bring them to their knees in prayer. The darkness represents your sins and how you are spiritually lazy in your apathy and arrogance. Remember that you are being tested here for a short time and you have little time to waste. Whether you are in good times or bad, you need to remember Me in your prayers, so I can keep you focused on your goal in Heaven. It does not matter how famous or how rich you become. In the end your test will be how much you loved Me and your neighbor. So be ever vigilant in prayer and ever watchful for My Coming, because you know not the hour."**

Later, I could see a compass (for making circles) among the trees of a forest. Mary came with her mantle and she said: "**My dear children, my old messages are coming to fruition. I told you that some clergy are on their way to perdition, even some in high places. This symbol that you are seeing in the compass represents the Masons. The Masons among the clergy will be leading the schism in the Church. Pray for your clergy in perdition that they will see their erring ways and convert back to my Son. Pray that Satan will not control your bishops and cardinals. Pray for Pope John Paul II that he may be strengthened to endure the coming trial. I will place my mantle over all who call on me in my Rosary. The Rosary is your weapon against all evil influences. Remain faithful to our Two Hearts and trust in my Son's victory over sin and death."**

**Wednesday, September 9, 1998:**

After Communion, I could see some people attending Mass in a church. Jesus said: "**My people, relish the moment that you can go to daily Mass and receive My Real Presence in Holy Communion. Many do not realize the treasure they have in the Mass. You concern yourselves with many things of the world, yet it is the spiritual treasures that last forever. A day is coming when the schism in My Church will make it difficult to find a valid Mass. Pray for your priests that they may follow the true teachings of My Church and not the lies of the Antipope. This evil pope will try and deceive My faithful. Pray and discern the spirit in everything he will proclaim as coming from the Church. He will try and change the proper Church teachings and eventually he will worship the Antichrist. Be ready, My faithful, to find underground Masses and leave this false church claiming My Name. This will be a difficult time to discern, since the evil one will be like an angel of light getting church members to follow him. Only follow Me and Pope John Paul II, who will be leading My remnant. Rejoice, for soon I will triumph over evil and you will then share in My Heaven on earth in My new Era of Peace.**"

**Thursday, September 10, 1998:**

After Communion, I could see a calm marsh and a calm coastline. This was followed by wind and rain on both. Jesus said: "**My people, I have told you how you will grow weary of the constant storms in your land. Each storm will exact its toll on your possessions and some lives will be lost. These punishments you are bringing on yourselves, because you are not repenting for your sins. It will not be long until the people see the connection between their sins and these storms. The financial burdens will bring many to their knees. Awake, America, from your sins or you will continue to face these storms of destruction. Seek My forgiveness in Confession and your souls will be cleansed. If you repent and make reparation, I will mitigate the damage of further storms. Come to Me in love, My children, for I would rather bring you My blessings, instead of My justice. You are the ones deciding your destiny. If you seek worldly desires, you will lose what little you have. If you seek heavenly treasures, I will bless you abundantly.**"

Later, at the prayer group, I could see President Clinton in lights seeking forgiveness. Jesus said: **"My people, as your president seeks forgiveness, let him seek My forgiveness as well for his sins. Everyone can seek My forgiveness, no matter how severe the sinner. I have told you since your president sent out his edicts to favor abortion that I would smite him. His heart has not changed, since he is still voting for partial birth abortion. All those who cause the death of My babies will pay dearly in this world and the next. Killing babies or encouraging it, is more severe than some of your president's lies. For this reason alone, he is being humiliated with My justice."**

I could see red blood being spewed from a man with a forked tongue. Jesus said: **"My people, the Antichrist is not long from taking power over your world. He, like Satan, has a taste for man's blood. He will try and martyr any of My faithful that he can get his hands on. He will continue to have abortions offered up in evil worship. He will cause battles all over the world, so he can gain power. All those who share in this death mentality will be in league with the Antichrist. But one day the blood of all evil people will flow as they are cast into Hell in utter defeat. Pray for peace and pray to stop the killing of all people. I will protect those who pray for My help."**

I could see Jesus on a narrow cross and the serpent was striking at Him. Jesus said: **"My people, since the moment that I died on the cross, Satan knew that I had gained victory over him. So do not be afraid of any evil. Call on My Name and I will come to your aid. Those who are faithful to Me have nothing to fear from the evil one. Do not be disheartened when evil seems to be winning some battles. Know that in the end, all evil will lose the war when I come in glory. Your suffering on earth will be brief, but the evil souls and evil spirits will suffer eternal torment in the flames of Hell."**

I could see Mary with a bright light around her and she was leading souls through a long tunnel toward Heaven. Mary said: **"My dear children, on my feast days I bring those souls up from Purgatory that are ready to come to Heaven. Do not forget these poor souls, especially your own relatives. The more Rosaries and Masses you have offered up for these souls, the** sooner they can be brought to Heaven. Thank you for your Rosaries tonight as I will give your intentions to my Son."

I could see hills upon hills of sand dunes. Jesus said: "My people, you have abused your fertile land for other purposes than growing crops. Because you have despoiled the land in your waste, much of your land will turn into deserts and dust bowls. This will be the beginning of your world famine. All of these consequences are coming from your own hands. Pray for My help in providing for your needs. I will multiply food and water for those who trust in My miracles."

I could see some white fences knocked down along with some trees on the ground. Jesus said: "My people, you have witnessed destruction and power outages throughout the year in many places. Still unless it happens in your own backyard, you are little influenced. As you carry your broken tree limbs and sit in darkness, remember when I told you that I would strip your possessions. As your pockets are affected, reality of My justice has to be recognized. Pray for My blessings to return, or you will drown in your sins."

I could see some flames burning over the ground. Jesus said: "My people, you have seen much damage from fires this year. You will continue to see flames in fires of brush, houses, and accidents. Again, My justice is being carried out by these cleansing flames. The searing heat of these flames is but a taste that your souls will suffer in Purgatory or Hell. Come to Me out of love or come to Me out of the fear of the flames of Hell. I am all merciful, but I am just as well. Come to My graces of Confession and your soul can rest with Me in the glory of Heaven."

### Friday, September 11, 1998:

After Communion, I could see a picture of President Clinton. Jesus said: "My people, many are quick to criticize your president for his affairs and his lies, but now others are publicly being scrutinized for the same problem. This morning's Gospel speaks of removing the plank out of your own eye before trying to remove the speck in your brother's eye. Remember when an adulterous woman was brought before Me. I asked that he who is without sin to cast the first stone. Eventually, all confessed to their own sins and I said to the woman: 'I forgive you, now go and sin no more.' Be careful not to be a hypocrite in professing your faith. It is very important not to give bad example. You all are sinners and are in need of repentance, so come to Me and I will forgive all of your sins. It is those who do not repent in their hearts that are condemned in their sins. Pray for the conversion of sinners who fail to admit their faults. You should have your souls prepared by contrition for the day that you will stand in judgment."

Later, at St. John the Evangelist Chapel, Susquehanna, Pa., I could see a priest raise a Bible and then my vision was focused on the tabernacle. Jesus said: "My people, look on My Word and My Real Presence in the Host as the most treasured gifts that I have given you. Through My Word you are given what has happened and what will come to be. My Word is a blueprint of how events will come about. Do not be fearful, for I have told you that I will be with you to the end of time. This is why it is very important that you preserve and protect My Real Presence in My Blessed Sacrament. It is by this Sacramental Presence that I can be seen and worshiped. Treasure the moments that you can adore Me in places of Perpetual Adoration. When you can no longer find a Mass or My Tabernacle, you can still call on Me in spiritual communion. During the Tribulation I will allow My angels to place My Most Precious Host miraculously on your tongue. I will not leave you orphans, but I will protect those faithful to Me, despite the temptations of the world and the Antichrist. Call on My Name and My protection will come into your midst. Remember that I will triumph over all evil and this is only a test of your endurance and your allegiance to Me."

**Saturday, September 12, 1998:**

At St. Cecilia's Church, Rockaway, N.J., after Communion, I could see an ornate kneeler where a couple was being married. Jesus said: "My people, when a man and woman are joined in marriage, they are bonded to each other and to Me in the Marriage Sacrament. At that moment, you make your vows before Me that each spouse will be faithful in love to each other. If you are to abide by these vows, the husband will not seek other women, nor should the wife seek other men. Divorce is so rampant in your country because many partners are selfish and do not seek to keep the marriage together. Your vows should be a life long contract, not just a piece of paper that you can tear up at your whim. It is this faith commitment that is missing in many relationships. Look to My love for My Church as an example for you to imitate. You may see failings in each other, but look to love each other despite these human flaws. Do not criticize each other's faults, but look to the good in each other to honor and love. Treat each other as your own body, because you are joined as one with Me. When you sin against each other, you are sinning against Me. So pray each day to preserve your marriages and reach out each day in love of your spouse. Do not let the flame of love go out, but preserve it as an eternal flame. Pray for all marriages that these families will remain united in My love. When your families break down, your whole society will break down as well. Love is everything in life, so follow Me in love in all that you do."

Later, at Leticia Villar's house, The Apostolate of the Holy Family in Bedminster, N.J., I could see people in the forest with a camera looking on. Jesus said: **"My people, I am asking you to have no fear, even when you are at My refuges in the Tribulation. I give you all of My blessings to provide for your protection. Pray for My help and I will multiply food for you and water to drink. In those days My angels will protect you from all evil men. These evil men will have difficulty in finding you and even if they should find you, they will not be able to enter My refuges. I will send you My heavenly manna and I will provide for your shelter. So relax in My rest and be assured that I will take care of all of your needs. Do not ever accept anything from the evil one. You do not need his food nor his jobs. Worship Me only and My love will be spread over all of My faithful. Trust in Me and your salvation will be assured."**

**Sunday, September 13, 1998:**

At St. Elizabeth's Church in Far Hills, N.J., after Communion, I could see a crucifix on an elevated casket. Then later the cross was gone with a door opened into an empty casket. Jesus said:

"My people, your time on earth is short. It is not long from your birth until you will be facing your judgment. You worry more about your existence in this short lifetime than you care about where you will spend your eternity. Being with Me in Heaven is your soul's desire. Anything, besides Me, will not bring you peace or rest. Your soul is an immortal spiritual being and it seeks to praise its Creator. You cannot deny these spiritual cravings to be with Me. That is why no matter how many of this world's possessions you have, you are not completely satisfied. My grace and My Presence are all that will satisfy your soul. Your life should be but one preparation for your eternal life. You cannot come to Heaven unless you come through Me. I have purchased your souls by My death on the cross, so I am the gatekeeper. But I do not force My love on anyone. I ask you to love and choose Me freely by your own free will. When you are gifted with faith, you can see how I love each of you with an infinite love. Your soul seeks Me because I am love personified. The devil will not love you, because he only seeks your destruction. I love you so much that I seek your love until your dying day. So live every day in My grace seeking to please Me in everything you do. Spending eternity in My love is why I created you. Return your praise to Me like the angels for your very opportunity to be alive."

Later, at Leticia Villar's house, Bedminster, N.J., I could see a red colored plane and other weapons of war. Jesus said: "**My people, many of your inventions have been made for war, or they were abused as weapons. You have made warplanes, warships, tanks, missiles, and even instruments to carry out abortions. All of these abuses were made for one purpose and that is to take lives in killing. Throughout history you have continued to make more fearsome weapons until now, with your nuclear weapons, you are threatening your very existence on earth. All of this desire for killing has come from Satan, because he brings only hate and death. I bring the exact opposite of love and eternal life. I tell you to seek only those things to share love with Me and your neighbor. Do not seek instruments of hate, death and destruction. Seek life because life comes from My hands. Evil men seek to kill. Taking of life is the most serious of sins** you can commit because you are violating My plans for these souls. So pray, My children, to stop wars and killing in abortions. Live to preserve life and not to take life. All life has a reason to live and My love reaches out to every soul. Live a life of love and avoid a life of hate."

**Monday, September 14, 1998:** (Triumph of the Cross) At St. Cecilia's Church, Rockaway, N.J., after Communion, I could see a cross at the Easter Vigil and then various crosses of different sizes. Jesus said: **"My people, I am showing you again how I have shaped every cross for each of you. If you were to choose among all crosses, you would pick your own. I came on the earth to deliver up My people, like Moses, only I came to give My life on the cross so you may be saved. I have asked each of you to take up your daily cross and carry it for Me. Some may want to refuse dealing with life's sufferings, but you will only make your cross heavier if you refuse. You can gain more graces by consecrating your sufferings up to Me each day. Otherwise, they would be wasted. As I was resurrected, I have shown you by example how one day you could be raised up to Heaven. Those who are faithful to My Commandments will receive this reward. So come, My children, and follow in My footsteps to Calvary. As Simon helped Me, I will help you if you seek My help. When you finally reach your destination, you can then share in My triumph."**

Later, at Adoration, I could see a steeple of a church with a white outline of light all around the edges. I then saw some bells ringing triumphantly. Jesus said: **"My people, I am anticipating for you a time after the Tribulation when everyone will be free to worship Me. The influence of evil men and evil spirits will be taken away, and with that all fear and hate will be removed as well. You are limited in your coming to perfection now, but in My new Jerusalem, you will be focused on living in My Divine Will. Your spirituality will be so raised, that loving Me at all times will be second nature. Follow Me in faith throughout the coming trial, and you will celebrate with Me in your new freedoms from evil. All Heaven will rejoice with you as you will share in My triumph over Satan and sin. My faithful will then live a** life of perfection as I intended life to be before Adam's fall. Prepare for this sharing of My love, as I purify the earth of all evil."

**Tuesday, September 15, 1998:** (Mother of Sorrows)

After Communion, I saw a statue of Mary in stone and then she came dressed in brown. Mary said: **"My dear children, I want you to join our Two Hearts in love and in suffering. Everything my Son, Jesus, had to suffer, I suffered with Him in my heart. I had to endure the injustice of my Son's death, yet I knew that it was for a greater good in saving all of mankind from their sins. Parents suffer pain in their hearts when their children suffer any injuries. It is that same shared pain that I suffered with my Son. Because all of you are joined in One Mystical Body, Jesus still suffers all of your hurts when you are in pain. As your heavenly mother, I reach out to each of you with my mantle of protection. Seek my help in the Rosary and I will console your difficulties. You all suffer pain in life and it is comforting for you to know that I stand by you to help you."**

Later, at Adoration, I could see a cobra standing to strike. Then it changed into a red rose and kept changing back and forth. Jesus said: **"My people, this vision represents those who are trying to undermine groups that are fighting against abortions. They act on one side as against abortion, but their deeds are the poison which is trying to give a bad name for those wanting to preserve life. These spies are devious in causing trouble and they are funded by evil people. Those who kill and cause damage, do not have their heart full of love. Instead, they spew the venom of hate and cannot sincerely want to preserve life. I have given you many examples of hypocrites when I spoke of good trees only bearing good fruit and bad trees only bearing bad fruit. Be suspicious of the origins of these building burners, for their works are only from the evil one. Taking of life can never justify an action to support a pro-life position."**

**Wednesday, September 16, 1998:**

After Communion, I could see a small opening on the side of a mountain. Then the stone facing seemed to cover up the opening so it could not be detected. Jesus said: **"My people, as the time to go** into hiding draws near, do not be fearful. I will provide a place of protection for you that will hide you from the evil men of that time. For some, My angels will lead you to caves in the hills. By My miraculous help, the evil people will not be able to see you. My angels will protect you from diseases and any physical harm. At the same time I will provide food, water, and shelter. Those at My refuges and caves will have nothing to fear and you will have plenty of time for prayer and preparation for My Era of Peace. Rejoice that I am watching out for My faithful, even while the Antichrist has his brief reign. Share My love for you by showing your love for all of those with you in hiding."

Thursday, September 17, 1998:

After Communion, I could see someone kneeling on a kneeler to receive Holy Communion on the tongue. Jesus said: "**My people, the woman in today's Gospel kissed My feet, washed them with her tears, dried them with her hair, and perfumed them for My burial. I forgave her sins because of her faith and reverence. I am a loving God and I reach out to help those who request My help in prayer. As in this vision, it is more proper to give honor to My Real Presence in the Mass. Those who kneel during the consecration and receive My Host on the tongue are like this woman giving Me heartfelt reverence. If you really recognized your loving God is present in the consecrated Host, you would kneel and bow in homage. When I come again, all mankind will bow in My Presence. Give honor and praise to Me before My Tabernacles and at Perpetual Adoration.**"

Later, at the prayer group, I could see an ornate ceremony as a new pope was being seated. Jesus said: "**My people, time is coming close for your present Pope John Paul II to be exiled. At that time, a cardinal with evil and liberal intentions will be elected pope. He will ease the position against sins of the flesh and violate My laws put forth by My Apostles. He will change many Church laws in the name of accommodation of other churches. Know that you should not follow this evil pope, who will lead you to the Antichrist's power. When this pope takes over the throne of St. Peter, get ready to flee into hiding. Do not stay at your homes, for they will come to take you to detention** centers to kill you if you delay. The Antichrist will try to force everyone to take the Mark of the Beast under pain of death."

I could see some Arabic symbols on a building and the people were seeking war. Jesus said: "My people, some Muslim leaders will continue to incite their people to take up arms in the Middle East. Several hot spots are ready to boil over in a war that could spread to more nations. Pray, My people, for peace in your world, because the hate of each other grows worse. Every act of killing will cause more killing until a vicious circle of wars will erupt. Once a major war starts, it may quickly lead to weapons of mass destruction."

I could see a light house at night and there was a vigil before the next major storm was to strike the coast. Jesus said: "My people, you have seen major devastation in your country, Mexico, China and now Japan. Are you yet realizing that these storms are testing you for a reason? Every country that has relied on its wealth instead of My help, is being tested with serious natural disasters. How long will it take for you to change your lives and seek My forgiveness? I have sent you many messages to wake up and repent. I will continue to strip you of your wealth until you fall on your knees in prayer. When all seems lost, many will turn to the Antichrist for help. He will fail also, but still many will trust him. Trust only in My help, for I will be the victor over all evil."

I could see some factory buildings and many laid off workers were rioting because they were being fired. Jesus said: "My people, as your world depression advances, many corporations will be laying off large numbers of workers. This will cause more chaos as these people will be desperate to pay their bills and feed their families. Many nation's infrastructures will collapse without enough tax money to pay for services. Your country will not be long to feel these same effects. As economic turmoil continues, your money systems will crash and the Antichrist will come on the scene to force a new electronic money using only chips in the hand or forehead. These conditions are ripe even now for eventual martial law."

I could see a strange, large bomb explosion at night which rose as one big plume, not as a mushroom cloud. It appeared to be more of a neutron bomb killing people with minimal destruction of buildings. Jesus said: **"My people, pray on your knees that such bombs may not be used. These evil men will use means to kill that will not destroy buildings and will allow occupation in a short time. Biological warfare could be used even by terrorists. Be prepared for new warfare that does not have battle lines, but threatens major cities. The devil is taking advantage of the cold hearts that want to vent their anger on their enemies. If these wars are not compromised, you may see a World War III threaten man's survival. Pray for My protection during this turmoil, and I will send My angels to win My battles."**

I could see a huge demon image spread over the night sky. Jesus said: **"My people, I have prepared you for an evil age that will reach its height in the time of the Antichrist's rule. This man will have superhuman powers to deceive man into worshiping him. You will witness an evil on the earth with more power than you have ever seen before. Without My help and your guardian angel, your soul could not withstand this power. But My power is over all evil and I will bring a calm as I calmed the waters of the sea. With My victory, Satan will be chained in Hell and My Era of Peace will follow."**

I could look out some windows in the city and there was no one walking around. Jesus said: **"My people, as a new warfare breaks out, you will see many new and old diseases being released among your cities. Because of an absence of vaccines or cures, many will die and food will be scarce. That is why going into the rural areas or My refuges will be necessary for your protection. At the caves and the white crosses, you will be healed from all diseases. This will be My mercy for those who are faithful. All other sinners without forgiveness will suffer agonizing deaths or a painful existence. Come to Me in love now, My children, before these events come upon you."**

**Friday, September 18, 1998:**

After Communion, I could see a large kettle of molten iron being poured. In another scene it was idle and empty. Jesus said: **"My people, many of your factories will have their workers cut back until some will close. As more mergers develop, there will be** fewer needs for skilled labor and management. Your people will be displaced in their jobs with only service jobs available. Many will lose their homes and the banks will fail that hold their mortgages. This will precipitate a circle of bankruptcies that will add to the world depression. All of these events will be leading up to the control of the world by the Antichrist. It is your spiritual bankruptcy that is worse than the loss of your money and your jobs. This is why all of your physical possessions are falling all around you. Without Me in your hearts, your material things will crumble in ruin. Turn yourself to My help and I will protect you from the evil ones in this coming trial."

At St. Thomas More Church, in Arlington, Virginia, I could see a man looking over someone in order to place the chip in their hand. I then could see a spiritual white light as interference of this electrical device. Jesus said: **"My people, man prides himself in all of his electrical marvels. These chips will be abused by the power of the Antichrist to control people's thoughts. He will send out communications to have people with the chips worship him. These systems will not be free from electrical interference. I will have My angels thwart the Antichrist's control, such that his agents will not be able to find My faithful. Heavenly interference will distract the evil people from doing anything harmful to those at My refuges. All of man's devices are vulnerable and I will take advantage of these failures to protect My people. Have faith and trust in My leading you to safety. You will walk past these evil men as the angel allowed St. Paul and My apostles to walk out of their cells unseen."**

**Saturday, September 19, 1998:**

At Our Lady of Good Counsel, Vienna, Virginia, after Communion, I could see a man standing beside a crucifix. Jesus said: **"My people, without My Resurrection and your belief in it, your faith would be in vain. It is only the body that dies at your death. Your soul lives on because of its immortality. By what you do in life, that will determine your soul's destination. Those who are faithful and have suffered on earth for their sins, are going to Heaven. Those who have yet to make reparation for their sins and are faithful will be purified in Purgatory. While** those who refuse to accept Me or do not seek forgiveness of their sins are asking for judgment to Hell. When I rose on Easter Sunday, I was showing you how your body will one day be reunited with your soul. You will also witness a glorified body of perfection. Those in this purified state will give Me honor and praise as My angels do. Rejoice in your resurrection when you will share eternal life with Me. Your soul was created to be with Me in Heaven. So your being with Me will be the fulfillment of your soul's desire."

Later, at St. Michael's Adoration, Annandale, Virginia, I could see a stage with about twenty rich leaders all dressed in black capes looking very sinister. Jesus said: "**My people, I am showing you the titans of business and finance. They are evil men because they have made a pact with the devil for their riches and power on earth. They have literally sold their souls for their glory on earth. They think when life is over that there is nothing after death. These men are living a fast life since they know their time is short. Satan is using this ruthless group to steal as much money from all of the rest of the world as they can. These men hold the purse strings of all of the major economic countries in the world. They will buy and sell people, even kill to keep their power. Remember when I told you, that there is nothing in this world that is worth losing your soul over. So, do not let Satan control your hearts or make gods out of money or any other idols. Keep your focus on loving Me and your neighbor so you have no time to be selfish. Seek only to gain in spiritual treasures and do not seek to let physical pleasures or physical treasures run your lives.**"

**Sunday, September 20, 1998:**

At St. Andrew's Church in Centerville, Virginia, after Communion, I could see a dark basement room with a safe in the wall and then it fell down into a deep pit. Jesus said: "**My people, you are faced with a choice in life to choose between a loving God or the cold idol of money. Elusive wealth of the world is not to be trusted. If you have plenty of money in the banks or stocks, do not think that you are secure in this world. Banks can fail through theft, bad times or bankruptcy. Your gold and coins** can become worthless when food is scarce. Your stocks can fall or your homes fall in value. All of this world's riches can corrode or disappear tomorrow. But heavenly treasures will last forever and will never corrode or dissipate. Those good deeds or contributions of time and money will be stored up. Those things that have been repaid or in other ways compensated, will not be stored up. That is why what you do in secret, My Father will reward you. Do not look for thanks or repayment, for you are already repaid here. It is to store treasure in Heaven without earthly praise that will be with you in the next life. So, come graciously to give of your time and earthly treasure to share that for Me and your neighbors. I read your soul's intention in all that you do, so come worship Me and thank Me for all that you have."

Later, at Adoration, I could see some entrance gates to an outdoor prison with fencing and barbed wire. I then saw thousands of people being processed in these camps right after their capture. Jesus said: "My people, I am showing you these active prison camps to bring reality to your understanding. All of these foreign troop movements and all of these camps were not set up unless they planned to use them. The evil men in your government are controlled by the One World people. They plan to initiate an emergency that would trigger martial law. It is under martial law that all of your executive orders would become effective. These people have planned lists of people to be killed so they would not interfere with the New World Order. Those with guns, those that are religious and those defiant of government control, are the people on these lists. I am preparing you, My people, so that you can go into hiding to avoid being killed in these death camps. These plans for your destruction and takeover are ready to be implemented soon. They have covered every detail, even to the cremation of the bodies. There is so much evidence available, it is a wonder that more people are not questioning their representatives. My power is greater that Satan's power and I have shown you how your angels will help you in this trial. Rely only on My providing of food and shelter and never take the evil one's Mark of the Beast or chip in your hand or forehead. Give allegiance only to Me and I will provide for your needs. This evil lot will soon be cast into Hell and you will rejoice in My new Era of Peace."

**Monday, September 21, 1998:** (St. Matthew)

After Communion, I could see a huge solid, silver metal wheel that was moving slowly. Jesus said: **"My people, there are many evil things going on in this evil age, yet there are many beautiful things as well. My Church moves very slowly at times, yet it is carrying out its mission of saving souls. The other side of My Church is the quiet strong hand that I supply to carry it on. My power is overwhelming as a large steamroller that just flattens evil as injustice is pushed aside by My justice. Do not credit Satan or evil people with any of their own power. Evil is insignificant before Me and I only allow its presence as a test of My faithful's faith. The evil one will not harm those who are faithful and whom I am protecting. You saw that Satan had no power over Me in the desert and the demons obeyed My every command. When I come again, you will see Satan and all the evil men and the evil spirits crushed under My power and chained in Hell. So have no fear of evil when My power is on your side. I am the Victor of the past, the present, and the future. Ask My help and I will go with you to bring many souls to Heaven. Reach out and be brave because you have My strength behind you."**

Later, at Adoration, I could see some laser beams or microwaves being pointed at some cars as they passed toll points on the highway. Jesus said: **"My people, beware of your electrical gadgets and all of the new reading devices. Your new toll transponders are another means for the One World people to track your activities. With these new passes they can determine patterns by your entrances and exits on all of the toll roads across your country. These same people already know your buying habits by what you charge. All of these new devices are said to speed up your transactions, but they have devious motives and plans to link all of this to the Mark of the Beast. This will be the most desirable means promoted to make life easy. In fact, all of these chips are being designed to give control over everyone by the Antichrist. You can refuse to be influenced by the Antichrist by** not using any electronic means for your transactions. Refuse to take the Mark of the Beast, even if it means not being able to buy and sell or enter a job. By relying on what I will provide for you, rather than the Antichrist, you will save your soul and not be influenced by the evil one. Prepare, My children, to go into hiding before they come to your house to force you to take the chip or go to a detention center. You are being given ample time and warning to understand how the Antichrist will run the New World Order. Pray for My help and your salvation will be won."

**Tuesday, September 22, 1998:**

After Communion, I could see an electrical cord sheared off and a stack of blankets inside some plastic covering. Jesus said: "**My people, your power outages continue and many are in need of shelter and bedding. When homes are damaged, the displacement of people causes painful losses. These storms are exacting more damage because I have withdrawn My blessings from you. Natural disasters are increasing in intensity and frequency. Are you not recognizing My hand in all of this? Your riches and greed will be brought low as many will experience financial losses. As your wallets are attacked, many will sit up and take notice. When your money is threatened, you will soon come to Me on your knees. Pray for My help and I will come to your assistance. In all of this experience you are seeing that you always need My help, and all of your means for survival are vulnerable to collapse. Hang on to what is everlasting for that will not be lost.**"

Later, at Adoration, I could see a man dressed in a purple coat with a strap diagonally across his chest carrying a rifle. Jesus said: "**My people, you are about to see another revolution in your country between the One World UN forces and those who do not want to give up their guns. A movement will start by the government to collect all the guns. This will start the confrontation. The One World people will try and remove as many of your army troops as possible out of the country. Then they will infiltrate the police forces with foreign police officers. The purpose is to get the police to collect the guns. Those in the police and National Guard will have to choose between fighting their own people or the foreign UN troops and foreign police. Once** there is no more opposition, they will then try and force the Mark of the Beast chips on everyone. So as My people go into hiding, you will be confronted with these skirmishes. I do not ask you to take up weapons for defense, because Satan encourages this killing. I do not condemn any one for self-defense, but I encourage letting My angels fight your battles by blinding your enemies. You will be protected at My refuges from any killing, so there is no need to kill anyone. Know that these things will be going on around you even as you leave for hiding. Share all of your food and it will continue to multiply. Fear not all of this killing, but trust in My Word to protect your souls. Keep your sacramentals on you for protection, and you will not need any other defense. Pray much during this trial which will test your faith dearly."

### Wednesday, September 23, 1998:

After Communion, I could see a strip of gold hanging across the highway. I then saw cars racing toward the gold but never reaching it. Jesus said: "My people, many are struggling each day in their workplace to reach out for as much money as they can get. This kind of wealth is elusive and futile for most. Even once you attain your goal, you change that goal for something better. These are never ending struggles because you never will be satisfied with only earthly possessions. I am telling you this so you should relax and be content with a normal pace of living. Your rush for fame and fortune will not satisfy you, so why be taken up with impossible and unnecessary goals. Pray to Me first and all that you need will be provided for you. Concentrate your focus on following My Will and I will satisfy your soul more than you ever could. It is My grace and love that will fill your heart and soul with all that you desire. If you live every day on a spiritual level to please Me, you will not be concerned over any physical riches. So live life to the fullest with Me and I will open your eyes to following My Divine Will."

### Thursday, September 24, 1998:

At St. Martin de Porres, Yorba Linda, California, after Communion, I could see a luxury car on a stage or an altar. Jesus said:

"My people, do not place the material things in your world ahead of Me as an idol. You are not here to live this life for yourself only. I am asking you to live this life for love of Me and love of your neighbor. Many have lived before you and some have lived for themselves following their own devices. It is not new under the sun that some do not want to follow My ways. You, My servant, know of your conversion experience and how I wanted you to serve Me. It is this gift of service to Me that I call everyone to change their lives. You, My faithful, are placed in the world, but you are not to be of the world. Pray, My children, for My direction and My leadership so you will be led to follow My Will. I show you a path to take up your daily cross and follow the narrow road to Heaven. Be persistent in following My ways and you will stay focused on My plan for your life."

Later, at Mom's House with Thuy, I could see hills and places of shelter. Jesus said: "My people, you are My remnant and I will be calling you to places of protection. Have trust in Me that My angels will provide for your needs during the Tribulation. This will be a refuge of protection guided by our Two Hearts. When people are brought here, it is necessary for everyone to be in fervent prayer. At that time do not worry if enough food will be there. I will multiply some food for you. So, be patient and do not be anxious. If food is low, you can always pray to Me for spiritual communion. My angels will bring you My Host on your tongue at your request. Some in the past have survived on only My Eucharist. You, too, will be able to live only on My Heavenly Manna. So, have no fear and trust in My protection. My shield of protection with My angels will prevent evil ones from harming you. Be patient but a short time and I will bring you to My Era of Peace. The reward for your faithfulness will far surpass your dreams when you witness My Jerusalem on earth."

**Friday, September 25, 1998:**

At St. Martin de Porres, Yorba Linda, California, after Communion, I could see a calm water and then sudden destruction. Jesus said: "**My people, you need to understand that time in this world**

J.                              T.

is fleeting and many things are changing. You are seeing in your
news, that at one time people are rich in their homes, but the
next moment a storm can destroy everything. You do not realize what lies in wait in your future, but do not get comfortable
with your possessions which may be gone tomorrow. There is a

time for joy and a time for sorrow. When you carry your cross, you will be faced with difficulties and with good times. In all that you do in life, call on My help to struggle through both your spiritual and physical testing. Your spiritual testing is more subtle than your physical testing. Sin is a part of the human experience and you must be prepared to accept the responsibility of your actions. Following My ways will be contrary to the desires of the body. But those who follow My Will will have the richest of rewards in Heaven. Your struggle to keep holy will not be in vain, for I will give you My blessings in return. Fight the good fight and you will win your salvation."

Later, at Mother of Mercy Shrine, Enumclaw, Washington, I could see Jesus anguishing in pain on the Cross. Jesus said: "My dear people, I am calling you in love from the cross. I am still suffering on the cross for your sins. Every time you sin, you are wounding Me again. I am suffering and sharing in everyone's physical pain, because you are a part of My Mystical Body. Pray and seek My graces in My sacraments so you will have the strength to do My Will. The less sins you commit, you are saving Me that pain. All of My suffering was the cost of redeeming souls. Use your own suffering and pain to offer them up for the reparation of your sins. By your suffering here, you can lessen your time in Purgatory. Help to share My love with others so they can be open to Me and open to their salvation. It is this bringing of souls to Me that I request of all of My followers. My love is a joyous love that needs to be shared with everyone. Mine is a contagious love that needs spreading. I am a jealous God and I seek all souls until their time of judgment. Live in My love every day and you will be preparing for the day that you will be absorbed into My Being as one."

**Saturday, September 26, 1998:**

At Mother of Mercy Shrine, Enumclaw, Washington after Communion I could see a manger with hay as at a stable. Jesus said: "My people, I am showing you where I was born in Bethlehem because I humbled Myself to be born in a cave. When you were born, you had nothing when you came into the world. By leaving everything behind to save your life, you are really preparing yourself to come into My new Era of Peace. You need to die to self in order to come to Heaven. So, when you are brought into hiding by your angel, this will help you in stripping yourself of your materialism. Those that accept the Antichrist and his pleasures will not be saved, because they lived for themselves instead of Me. Even though the Tribulation will be difficult to endure, it does have a hidden blessing in stripping you willingly. If you remained in your comfort and luxury without testing, how else would your love for Me be manifested? If you love Me, you will follow My Will in all I am asking you to do."

Later, at Mother of Mercy Shrine, Enumclaw, Washington, I could see a stand of wheat sitting on an altar at the harvest. Jesus said: **"My people, I am coming to you in harvest season to remind you of My coming for your souls. I told My Apostles that they would now be fishers of men. So now I speak to all the harvest masters to gather My wheat into My barn, while the chaff and tares shall be thrown into the fire. I have given you My mercy in allowing the tares to grow up with the wheat. You have been graced with My mercy in having more time to repent and be saved. I am asking My faithful as the wheat, to reach out to save the tares who are the souls that may be lost if they do not change their lives. My judgment is coming close, so prepare your souls and those of your neighbor to receive Me. My infinite love and mercy are being poured out on My people. Listen to My call and be saved."**

**Sunday, September 27, 1998:**

At Adoration, I could see a large aircraft carrier and it carried a red star on it coming from Red China. Jesus said: **"My people, there is another growing danger in the East that wants to assume power as Russia is weak. Mainland China will extend its power by army and a built up navy to try and take more territory such as Taiwan. They are eager to build up their empire as they fool the western nations into helping them to spread their version of communism. Communism is not dead and Red China is resuming its goal for world conquest. The subtle peace you have now is just a facade to cover the current power struggles going on between the East and the West. You have so many elements in the** world that are all struggling for military control. In some aspects your country in America is becoming weaker and you will soon lose your world power status. Many evil forces are at work to tear down your country's defenses so you can be taken over. Your demise will come unless you repent of your sins of abortion and your many sins of the flesh. Pray much that your people will repent and change their lives before it is too late."

**Monday, September 28, 1998:**

After Communion, I could see a crown of thorns on the back wall of a church. All the statues, the Tabernacle, and everything was stripped. Jesus said: **"My people, the time of your schism in My Church is coming soon. My Pope son, John Paul II, will be exiled and the laity and clergy will have to decide whether to follow the Antipope or My Remnant Church. No longer will I tolerate the lukewarm. You will either love Me or not. Those that are just giving Me lip service will be the weak that get deceived by the Antipope. Worship only Me and follow what My Apostles passed on to you. Do not follow the Antipope who will mislead you to worship the Antichrist. This will be a true test of your faith and only the strong are going to save their souls. Pray that these weak souls will strengthen themselves to take a stand for Me. Otherwise, they are going to be sifted by evil influences. Now is the time to grow stronger in your faith, because the spiritual storms are on the horizon."**

Later, at Adoration, I could see Jesus in a white tunic with His arms raised offering up praise to His Father in Heaven. Jesus said: **"My people, I am calling your attention to My authority and Mine alone. Do not give worship to any alien god or any one claiming to be Me. Your age is moving deeper into apostasy where those in teaching authority are no longer teaching the truth. Everyone, even popes, bishops, or priests are commanded to teach My Word in Scripture and to teach the following of My Commandments. If someone teaches that masturbation, fornication or homosexual acts are not serious sins, then do not believe in their teaching. If someone says abortion or euthanasia is not a serious sin, then do not believe their teaching. If someone demands you to take the Mark of the Beast or praise** the Antichrist, then again do not believe their teaching as well. I am giving you this clear directive to prepare you for the coming Tribulation and the evil false witness who will assume the chair of St. Peter. I will protect My Remnant Church, but those who commit murder, sins of the flesh, or worship of anyone other than Me, will have to stand in judgment for their errors."

**Tuesday, September 29, 1998:** (Archangels Michael, Gabriel, Raphael)

After Communion, I could see St. Michael as he was casting Satan down into a dark abyss. St. Michael said: **"I am Michael and I stand before God. Beyond any doubt, I want to assure you that there is a Heaven and there is a Hell. Also, it is important to know that the devil does exist in the entity of an evil angel called Satan. It is one of his tricks to try and make people believe that he does not exist. This is why it is important to know that your weakened condition is at risk from sin every day. Satan never sleeps and you will be tempted to sin at any time. Your guardian angel is with you to assist you in doing good things and to protect you from the evil one. You need to have your spiritual guard up every day because you are always in a battle of good and evil where the prize is your soul. Jesus and the devil are pursuing you at all times. Give in to your Savior who loves you and detest the evil one who hates you. By following Jesus' Will for you and avoiding temptations, you will win the battle. Seek Jesus in prayer and He will send you His graces."**

Later, at Adoration, I could see a tunnel with lights on it as a sewer tunnel with water rushing through it. I then saw up above a very windy scene from a major storm and then many little bugs walking around. Jesus said: **"My people, I am showing you another aftermath of your current storms. As rain and flooding occurs from these storms, they will cause many sewage lines to release toxic wastes into your streams. There is a strong chance of forming diseases and possible epidemics from this outbreak of bacteria and viruses. Prepare, My people, for your physical testing is increasing and your spiritual situation is reflected in the violence of your storms. Many of these storms will add to your financial woes as jobs and taxes will be affected. As more**

Josyp Terelya
1998

and more layoffs occur, there will be a major disruption in jobs and income that will overwhelm any state or government aid. Be forewarned of your coming instability which will lay the groundwork for martial law. I will bring you through this evil age and protect you from all of the Antichrist's control."

**Wednesday, September 30, 1998:**

After Communion, I could see some very high mountains and a plane passed over the mountains and into the sunset. Jesus said:

"My people, your country is passing into the sunset to indicate that it will soon meet its demise. Your people in the past were industrious and God-fearing. Today, your technology has become a god ready for a precipitous fall, because you have turned your back on My Commandments for life. Your morals are a shambles and your lifestyles are an abomination. You have made a mockery of My plan of marriage between husband and wife. When you have marriages of the same sex and multiple divorces, how is your society to stand? I tell you, for your sins of abortion and your sins of the flesh, your country is destined for destruction. Once your economy falls and your defenses fail, your enemies will consume you. You have brought this judgment upon yourselves, because you failed to repent of your sins and change your lives. You have not learned from history which has shown that most great nations have fallen from within when their morals fell into a decadent society. Pray, My children, for your country to turn around or it may soon fall into ruin."

# Prepare for the Great Tribulation and the Era of Peace

# Index

abortion groups
    undermined by clinic bombs (Jesus) — 9/15/98
abortion mentality
    coming, medical profession (Jesus) — 8/5/98
abortions
    pray to stop (Jesus) — 8/29/98
Adam and Eve
    cast from Garden of Eden (Jesus) — 7/16/98
African bombing
    foretelling of terrorists action (Jesus) — 8/6/98
Alpha & Omega
    home now and in Heaven (Jesus) — 7/18/98
America
    awake from sins (Jesus) — 9/10/98
    becoming a mission land (Jesus) — 7/9/98
    decadent society cause ruin (Jesus) — 9/30/98
    in darkness of sin (Jesus) — 9/3/98
    marching to its own funeral (Jesus) — 9/3/98
    pray or fall (Jesus) — 8/23/98
    to lose world status (Jesus) — 9/27/98
    wake up, days are numbered (Jesus) — 7/4/98
    will be ruined without God (Jesus) — 8/28/98
    will fall soon in ruin (Jesus) — 8/17/98
    without God, will fail (Jesus) — 7/9/98
angels
    marking cross on foreheads (Jesus) — 7/3/98
    need spiritual guard up (St. Michael) — 9/29/98
    protect us (Jesus) — 7/21/98
Antichrist
    about to assume power (Jesus) — 7/28/98
    chaos causing takeover (Jesus) — 8/6/98
    control of food, jobs, money (Jesus) — 7/7/98
    given base of control (Jesus) — 8/24/98
    has taste for killing (Jesus) — 9/10/98
    mind control, attractions (Jesus) — 7/30/98
    perfoms illusions by satellite (Jesus) — 7/27/98
    stage set by famine, war (Jesus) — 7/17/98
    superhuman powers (Jesus) — 7/11/98
    superhuman powers, stopped (Jesus) — 9/17/98
    to come to power in chaos (Jesus) — 7/26/98
Antipope
    destroy Church from within (Jesus) — 7/24/98
    reigns over churches (Jesus) — 9/3/98
    to ease sins of the flesh (Jesus) — 9/17/98
    will deceive lukewarm (Jesus) — 9/28/98
apathy
    lazy in good times (Jesus) — 9/8/98
Apparition sites
    hiding places from Antichrist (Mary) — 8/6/98
Assumption
    sharing her resurrection (Mary) — 8/15/98
avarice
    do not desire money for itself (Jesus) — 8/18/98
bad habits
    change by grace and prayer (Jesus) — 8/27/98
Baptism
    washes away Original Sin (Jesus) — 7/28/98
battle of good and evil
    challenged to live one's faith (Jesus) — 7/17/98
    fight to save souls (Jesus) — 7/20/98
beatific vision
    infinite love and peace (Jesus) — 8/31/98
Bello Wedding
    uniting hearts (Jesus) — 8/22/98
Bible
    blueprint of events (Jesus) — 9/11/98
    living last book, Revelation (Jesus) — 7/28/98
bishops and cardinals
    have heavy responsibility (Jesus) — 9/6/98
bishops
    errors, authority, obedience (Jesus) — 9/28/98
    need prayers to stop pride (Jesus) — 8/19/98
bishops, erring
    do not follow errors, justice (Jesus) — 8/19/98
Blessed Sacrament
    give honor and reverence (Jesus) — 7/23/98
    give proper respect (Jesus) — 7/9/98

Blessed Sacrament visits
   take time in schedule for (Jesus)    8/9/98
bomb, nuclear
   neutron bomb, biological war (Jesus)    9/17/98
Burke, Tom
   message for family, friends (Tom Burke)   7/16/98
business leaders
   steal people's money, kill (Jesus)    9/19/98
cars
   fuel to be scarce (Jesus)    7/2/98
   use older vehicles for hiding (Jesus)    7/23/98
caves and healing
   healing waters (Jesus)    8/14/98
caves
   carved out in mountains (Jesus)    8/6/98
   healing water in grotto (Jesus)    7/21/98
caves protected
   angels protect from harm (Jesus)    9/16/98
chastisements vs. sin
   lose possessions, God's Will (Jesus)    7/30/98
children
   be examples of faith for (Jesus)    7/8/98
   teach the faith (Jesus)    7/11/98
children to visit Jesus
   encourage adoration (Jesus)    8/9/98
children
   victims of day care mentality (Jesus)    9/3/98
China
   extending its power (Jesus)    9/27/98
chips in the hand
   electrical interference, angels (Jesus)    9/18/98
choices
   for Heaven or Hell (Jesus)    7/16/98
church buildings
   keep statues and crosses (Jesus)    7/22/98
church and state
   distorted view of separation (Jesus)    7/4/98
churches closed
   from religious persecution (Jesus)    8/4/98
churches
   new buildings are colder (Jesus)    7/27/98

class struggle
   through job losses (Jesus)    7/26/98
clergy
   pray for them (Jesus)    9/6/98
Clinton
   all sinners need repentance (Jesus)    9/11/98
   disasters from abortion stand (Jesus)    8/14/98
   humiliated for abortion stand (Jesus)    9/10/98
   spouses need to be faithful (Jesus)    9/12/98
cobra vs. red rose
   death not a pro-life position (Jesus)    9/15/98
comet of chastisement
   already on its way to earth (Jesus)    8/21/98
communism
   controlled by monied people (Jesus)    8/28/98
   is not dead (Jesus)    9/27/98
   sponsored by One World people (Jesus)    9/3/98
conception
   soul gets spirit of life (Jesus)    9/5/98
Confession
   cleanses sin (Jesus)    7/28/98
   contemplate sins (Jesus)    8/11/98
   renews beauty of soul (Jesus)    8/30/98
   serious sins not taught (Jesus)    8/20/98
Confession, frequent
   no haste, contrite heart (Jesus)    8/11/98
Consecration
   miracle of daily Mass (Jesus)    7/6/98
corporal works of mercy
   good example to others (Jesus)    7/31/98
courts
   abuses of evidence, witness (Jesus)    8/13/98
creation
   give praise and glory to God (Jesus)    7/16/98
   is good, but abused (Jesus)    7/13/98
criticism and gossip
   replace with joy and love (Jesus)    9/2/98
cross, daily
   road to Calvary wins Heaven (Jesus)    9/14/98
daily Mass
   greatest gift (Jesus)    9/9/98

death mentality
  in war and abortion (Jesus) — 8/29/98
death, short life
  do not love worldly things (Jesus) — 8/21/98
demon image in sky
  evil time of Antichrist (Jesus) — 9/17/98
depression, economic
  history repeats itself (Jesus) — 9/3/98
desecration
  of statues and icons (Jesus) — 7/23/98
detention centers
  death camps, creamations (Jesus) — 9/20/98
devil worship
  dealing principalities, powers (Jesus) — 8/13/98
disease
  weapon for population control (Jesus) — 8/12/98
diseases, new and old
  new warfare on cities (Jesus) — 9/17/98
Divine Will
  be humble and repent (Jesus) — 7/15/98
  conform your will to Mine (Jesus) — 7/25/98
  let Jesus mold us to (Jesus) — 8/29/98
  our goal for Heaven (Jesus) — 9/3/98
door to hearts
  replace pride with Jesus (Jesus) — 8/8/98
driving annoyances
  slow life down, be patient (Jesus) — 8/19/98
earthquakes
  trust in angels in safe havens (Jesus) — 8/12/98
economies chaotic
  signs for Antichrist (Jesus) — 8/31/98
economies
  ready to collapse (Jesus) — 9/3/98
elevator
  need direction first (Jesus) — 8/10/98
Era of Peace
  everything provided (Jesus) — 7/16/98
  follow Divine Will, 2nd nature (Jesus) — 9/14/98
  living in the Divine Will (Jesus) — 9/4/98
  new Jerusalem (Jesus) — 7/2/98
  prepares yourself for Heaven (Jesus) — 9/26/98

errors
  forfeit authority & obedience (Jesus) — 9/28/98
eternal destination
  man created to be in Heaven (Jesus) — 9/13/98
euthansia
  genocide made acceptable (Jesus) — 8/5/98
evangelize
  Gospel message (Jesus) — 7/3/98
evil's power
  insignificant to God's power (Jesus) — 9/21/98
factories to close
  will cause banks to fail (Jesus) — 9/18/98
faith
  be humble and simple (Jesus) — 7/14/98
  have firm foundation for (Jesus) — 7/7/98
famine
  food and water rationed (Jesus) — 7/19/98
  will test the world (Jesus) — 7/17/98
famine to cause riots
  go into hiding as riots start (Jesus) — 8/20/98
Federal Reserve, bankers
  to take control of world (Jesus) — 9/3/98
feminists
  extremists ruin families (Jesus) — 9/3/98
fires in Florida
  stripped of materialism (Jesus) — 7/4/98
fires
  punishment for sins (Jesus) — 7/5/98
  taste of Hell or Purgatory (Jesus) — 9/10/98
flooding
  seek high ground (Jesus) — 8/27/98
Florida, fires in
  stripped of materialism (Jesus) — 7/4/98
food and water
  store now (Jesus) — 7/19/98
food multiplied
  to be shared at refuges (Jesus) — 8/20/98
forehead crosses
  will detect spies without (Jesus) — 8/13/98
future saints
  prayer, fasting, & good works (Jesus) — 8/11/98

genuflecting

    give glory to God (Jesus) — 7/10/98

    gives honor and glory (Jesus) — 9/5/98

germ warfare

    spread by military (Jesus) — 9/1/98

glorified bodies

    will be had in Heaven (Jesus) — 8/6/98

gold, frankincense, myrrh

    foretell Era of Peace (Jesus) — 7/12/98

Good Samaritan

    in physical & spiritual needs

        (Mother Cabrini) — 7/12/98

guardian angels

    assigned at parents' wedding (Jesus) — 9/5/98

    provide food and shelter (Jesus) — 9/3/98

    will lead us into hiding (Jesus) — 7/2/98

harvest masters

    gather wheat and tares (Jesus) — 9/26/98

healing

    have faith and trust (Mary) — 7/23/98

healing miracles

    going on even today (Mary) — 8/5/98

healings

    at luminous crosses, caves (Jesus) — 9/1/98

hearts open

    advance in spirituality (Jesus) — 8/8/98

Heaven

    eternal now, young forever (Jesus) — 7/6/98

    has different levels (Jesus) — 7/15/98

    will I be bored? All praising (Jesus) — 8/31/98

Heaven vs. Hell

    die to self, follow God's Will (Jesus) — 8/21/98

heavenly food

    satisfies soul more (Jesus) — 8/3/98

heavenly treasures

    secret deeds, not repayment (Jesus) — 9/20/98

Hell

    fires a preparation for (Jesus) — 7/5/98

Hell on earth

    fire, scorpions, plagues (Jesus) — 7/18/98

Hell on earth for lost

    evil cleansed from the earth (Jesus) — 8/21/98

hiding places

    food, water, shelter provided (Jesus) — 9/16/98

hiding

    refuges or caves (Jesus) — 9/4/98

hiding time

    when Pope John Paul II exiled (Jesus) — 9/17/98

Holy Communion

    no mortal sin in receiving (Jesus) — 8/3/98

Holy Communion, tongue

    reverence for Real Presence (Jesus) — 9/17/98

Holy of Holies

    reverence, Ark of Covenant (Jesus) — 9/5/98

Holy Spirit

    year dedicated to (Holy Spirit) — 7/20/98

holy places & shrines

    graces of protection (Jesus) — 7/23/98

homes

    have religious pictures (Jesus) — 7/6/98

Hosts

    reflection of love (Jesus) — 7/23/98

inventions for killing

    weapons of war threaten life (Jesus) — 9/13/98

Iraq military threat

    miscalculation, cause of war (Jesus) — 8/6/98

Jakus, Irena

    gratitude for pictures (Jesus) — 7/23/98

Jesus' victory

    past, present, & future (Jesus) — 9/21/98

Job

    tested by My blessings (Jesus) — 7/28/98

jobs

    are disappearing for greed (Jesus) — 7/16/98

Jonah

    symbolic 40 days now (Jesus) — 7/22/98

judgment

    separate wheat and tares (Jesus) — 8/23/98

killing from Satan

    love and life from God (Jesus) — 9/13/98

leaders cause wars
  greed and power reasons (Jesus) — 8/7/98
life is a test
  of loving God and neighbor (Jesus) — 9/8/98
life
  is most precious gift (Jesus) — 9/7/98
life style
  seek calm, not to be busy (Jesus) — 7/9/98
love
  share with everyone (Jesus) — 9/25/98
lukewarm
  lifeless, neither hot nor cold (Jesus) — 7/26/98
Mark of the Beast
  designed to control people (Jesus) — 9/21/98
  do not take it (Jesus) — 9/3/98
  owners to suffer Hell on earth (Jesus) — 7/18/98
  take or imprisoned, tortured (Jesus) — 7/2/98
  vulnerable to interference (Jesus) — 9/18/98
marriage mockery
  same sex, divorces, US ruin (Jesus) — 9/30/98
marriage
  need to be preserved in love (Jesus) — 9/12/98
  union, gift of love to spouses (Jesus) — 7/29/98
martial law
  after storms & layoffs (Jesus) — 9/29/98
  fiat tyranny (Jesus) — 7/4/98
  implement executive orders (Jesus) — 9/20/98
martyrdom
  pain will be softened (Jesus) — 7/23/98
martyrs
  in persecution (Jesus) — 7/21/98
  raised up in Era of Peace (Jesus) — 7/18/98
  to come in Tribulation (Jesus) — 8/10/98
  witnesses of faith (Jesus) — 7/23/98
Mary and Martha
  faith and trust (Jesus) — 7/19/98
Mary
  fewer visits, purpose done (Mary) — 7/23/98
Masons
  among clergy (Mary) — 9/8/98
  sharing wealth is real value (Jesus) — 8/13/98

Mass
  participate with heart (Jesus) — 7/26/98
material things lost
  do not worship possessions (Jesus) — 7/30/98
materialism
  stripped of possessions (Jesus) — 7/2/98
media
  censored to protect evil ones (Jesus) — 8/13/98
mercy
  given more time to repent (Jesus) — 9/26/98
mercy killing
  death culture promoted (Jesus) — 8/5/98
mercy, time of
  justice postponed for prayer (Jesus) — 7/30/98
messages
  re-read in light of events (Mary) — 9/6/98
messengers
  abused for telling the truth (Jesus) — 7/31/98
miracles
  gift of faith (Jesus) — 7/6/98
  witness supernatural events (Mary) — 8/5/98
money and excesses
  do not be rich for yourself (Jesus) — 8/18/98
money
  greed to be rich (Jesus) — 7/16/98
money vs. God
  elusive wealth not trusted (Jesus) — 9/20/98
Moses
  greater than Moses here (Jesus) — 9/5/98
Mother Cabrini Shrine
  love God and neighbor (Mother Cabrini) — 7/12/98
Mother of Sorrows
  suffered loss of Jesus (Jesus) — 9/15/98
music
  His gift to us (Jesus) — 9/4/98
Muslim leaders
  leading people to war (Jesus) — 9/17/98
natural disasters
  defy One World people (Jesus) — 8/13/98
  increase intensity, frequency (Jesus) — 9/22/98
  rain, fire, droughts (Jesus) — 7/2/98

**Prepare for the Great Tribulation and the Era of Peace**

New Age
    pagan gods of the earth (Jesus)      8/15/98
New Jerusalem
    evil influence removed (Jesus)      9/14/98
New World Order
    cannot conquer will, spirit (Jesus)      7/17/98
    control banks and stocks (Jesus)      8/24/98
    destruction, persecution (Jesus)      8/17/98
    killing lists, religious, patriots (Jesus)      9/20/98
    threats via food & medicine (Jesus)      8/12/98
nuclear encounter
    hold up hands in prayer (Jesus)      7/30/98
nuns
    contemplative, assist dying (Jesus)      8/6/98
    encouraged in faith (St. Therese)      8/16/98
One World People
    behind evil crimes (Jesus)      8/27/98
    make us a police state (Jesus)      9/3/98
    control food (Jesus)      7/19/98
    doing away with freedoms (Jesus)      7/4/98
    leaders selling out to (Jesus)      7/7/98
    pillaging our wealth (Jesus)      7/16/98
    take advantage of shortages (Jesus)      7/2/98
One World Religion
    worship sun, moon, earth (Jesus)      8/15/98
orders of nuns visited
    continue dedication to vows (St. Therese) 8/16/98
patience
    control your temper (Jesus)      8/19/98
peace
    prayers to stop killing (Jesus)      8/4/98
police
    avoid working with UN (Jesus)      8/13/98
police state
    by UN and New World Order (Jesus)      8/14/98
police, foreign infiltrators
    with UN, capture resistors (Jesus)      9/22/98
Pope John Paul II
    follow his teachings (Jesus)      9/6/98
    his leaving to trigger schism (Jesus)      8/20/98
    pray to strengthen (Mary)      9/8/98

    stay faithful to his teachings (Jesus)      7/24/98
    will be exiled (Jesus)      9/28/98
popes
    errors, authority, obedience (Jesus)      9/28/98
possessions
    may be lost (Jesus)      9/25/98
possessions stripped
    by destruction & power loss (Jesus)      9/10/98
    by storms and finances (Jesus)      8/31/98
prayer
    be persistent and humble (Jesus)      8/27/98
    listen for God's plan (Jesus)      7/9/98
prayer for peace
    African action, cycle of killing (Jesus)      8/20/98
presidential election
    fortunate to have another (Jesus)      7/4/98
pride
    proud are humbled (Jesus)      8/2/98
priests
    errors, authority, obedience (Jesus)      9/28/98
principalities & powers
    fight with angel (Holy Spirit)      7/20/98
priorities
    follow Jesus on narrow road (Jesus)      8/10/98
prophets & messengers
    truth, humility, no money (Jesus)      7/9/98
prophets
    not to criticize, God's duty (Jesus)      7/31/98
    persecution (Jesus)      7/2/98
protection
    by angels at refuges (Jesus)      7/3/98
    for those with faith and trust (Jesus)      7/16/98
psalms
    songs of praise (Jesus)      9/4/98
Purgatory
    to suffer on earth is better (Jesus)      9/25/98
    offer your suffering now (Jesus)      9/3/98
purification
    to perfect us for Heaven (Jesus)      9/3/98
Queenship of Mary
    follow His Will (Mary)      8/22/98
    Virgin birth, sinless gift (Mary)      8/22/98

Real Presence
    adoration (Jesus)    9/11/98
    Eucharist not just a meal (Jesus)    7/30/98
    not being taught (Jesus)    7/27/98
refuge
    hard life but no fear (Jesus)    8/14/98
refuge of protection
    Mom's house (Jesus)    9/24/98
refuges
    protection from evil men (Jesus)    9/12/98
    trust in food, shelter provided (Jesus)    8/12/98
renovations
    of hearts, not altars (Jesus)    7/14/98
repent
    for sins of abortion and flesh (Jesus)    9/27/98
Resurrection
    foretold in Transfiguration (Jesus)    8/6/98
    without it, faith in vain (Jesus)    9/19/98
retaliation in war
    may cause an escalation (Jesus)    8/20/98
reverence
    bow, genuflect to praise God (Jesus)    9/17/98
    display pictures & statues (Jesus)    7/14/98
    proper Church behavior (Jesus)    7/10/98
revolution in America
    patriots vs. UN, foreign cops (Jesus)    9/22/98
rich leaders
    made pact with the devil (Jesus)    9/19/98
    will lose their possessions (Jesus)    8/13/98
Russia
    communism will return (Jesus)    9/3/98
    controlled by atheism (Jesus)    8/28/98
sacramentals
    protection from evil (Jesus)    7/23/98
sacraments
    fountain of grace (Jesus)    7/9/98
    strength to do Divine Will (Jesus)    9/25/98
    strengthen against evil (Jesus)    8/23/98
sacrifice of Mass
    unbloody re-enactment (Jesus)    7/30/98
safe haven and caves
    protected from diseases (Jesus)    9/1/98

safe havens
    mantle of protection (Mary)    8/6/98
saints
    all are able to be one (Jesus)    7/2/98
    St. Clare, all can be saints (Jesus)    8/11/98
Satan will lose
    have no fear of evil (Jesus)    9/10/98
satellites
    signs and wonders, Antichrist (Jesus)    7/27/98
Scarantino Wedding
    Sacrament of Marriage (Jesus)    9/5/98
schism
    coming soon in Church (Jesus)    9/28/98
    go to underground Masses (Jesus)    9/3/98
    know old Bibles & catechism (Jesus)    8/25/98
    pray for clergy (Mary)    9/8/98
Scripture
    inspired by the Holy Spirit (Jesus)    7/15/98
    interpreted by the Church (Jesus)    7/15/98
Second Coming
    prepare for (Mary)    9/6/98
    prepare souls now (Jesus)    7/22/98
    triumph over the earth (Jesus)    7/12/98
separation, church&state
    ruled by madness (Jesus)    8/28/98
serve
    with humble, contrite hearts (Jesus)    8/29/98
service
    in world, not of it (Jesus)    9/24/98
servicemen
    avoid working with UN (Jesus)    8/13/98
sewage with storms
    causes disease, epidemics (Jesus)    9/29/98
shame, no sense of
    for sins of the flesh (Jesus)    7/29/98
sharing
    share possessions (Jesus)    8/2/98
Shroud of Turin
    proof of Resurrection (Jesus)    7/3/98
signs
    asked for, yet not believed (Jesus)    7/20/98

## Prepare for the Great Tribulation and the Era of Peace

signs of End Times
    floods, fires, earthquakes (Jesus)    7/9/98
signs of times
    violence reflected in weather (Jesus)    8/26/98
sin
    accept responsibility (Jesus)    9/25/98
sins
    confess, do not cover up (Jesus)    7/9/98
sins of the flesh
    serious sins (Jesus)    7/1/98
skull & crossbones
    battle of good and evil (Jesus)    8/13/98
smart cards
    preparation for chips in hand (Jesus)    7/2/98
soul's destination
    determined by faith (Jesus)    9/19/98
soul, immortal
    satisfied only in God (Jesus)    9/13/98
souls in Purgatory
    need more Rosaries, Masses (Mary)    9/10/98
St. Martha
    role model for women (Jesus)    7/29/98
St. Michael
    devil and Hell do exist (St. Michael)    9/29/98
St. Peter
    1st pope with Holy Spirit (Jesus)    7/7/98
St. Thomas
    doubted Resurrection (Jesus)    7/3/98
statue, Corpus Christi, Texas
    miracle in hearts (Jesus)    8/28/98
statues and icons
    desecration in persecution (Jesus)    7/23/98
statues and pictures
    in homes and churches (Jesus)    9/1/98
stealth weapons
    Antichrist's, will not work (Jesus)    8/13/98
stock market
    collapse with greed (Jesus)    7/16/98
storms and fires
    chastisements for sins (Jesus)    8/23/98

storms
    continue to bring us to knees (Jesus)    8/25/98
    financial losses, get attention (Jesus)    9/22/98
    pray to mitigate (Jesus)    8/27/98
    punishment for not repenting (Jesus)    9/10/98
    wealthy humbled, disasters (Jesus)    9/17/98
storms to get worse
    link of sins to lost blessings (Jesus)    8/6/98
suffering
    do not waste pain (Jesus)    7/31/98
teaching errors
    stand up for Church laws (Jesus)    8/20/98
technology
    trust more in God's power (Jesus)    7/30/98
terrorism
    never justified (Jesus)    8/27/98
terrorist bombs
    African bombing foretold (Jesus)    8/6/98
terrorist's activity
    fear is not worth martial law (Jesus)    8/20/98
testing
    of rude people and jobs (Jesus)    8/16/98
Titanic
    failure of man, God's success (Jesus)    7/30/98
toll passes
    patterns by entrances, exits (Jesus)    9/21/98
treasures
    seek those of Heaven (Jesus)    8/27/98
tribulation
    prepare for testing (Jesus)    8/16/98
    time of testing (Jesus)    9/26/98
Triumph of Cross
    Jesus came to deliver man (Jesus)    9/14/98
TV distractions
    brainwashes children (Jesus)    8/9/98
TV programs
    evil babysitter (Jesus)    7/11/98
Two Hearts
    shared pain in death (Jesus)    9/15/98
UN troops
    seeking removal of guns (Jesus)    9/22/98

underground Masses
    no more public worship (Jesus)    8/4/98
United Nations
    work with One World People (Jesus)    8/24/98
vaccines
    means to spread viruses (Jesus)    8/13/98
violence
    on TV and killings (Jesus)    8/29/98
war
    control your responses (Jesus)    8/27/98
    do not let evil cause killings (Jesus)    9/7/98
    ethnic & religious causes (Jesus)    8/7/98
    pray for peace (Jesus)    7/9/98
Warning
    remove TVs after (Jesus)    8/9/98
water to be saved
    water at risk of control (Jesus)    8/20/98
wealth
    will not satisfy your soul (Jesus)    9/23/98
weapons against faithful
    stealth weapons inactivated (Jesus)    8/13/98
weapons, mass destruct
    could end man's existence (Jesus)    8/4/98
weather
    disasters as signs (Jesus)    7/5/98
wedding feast
    has our places prepared (Jesus)    8/24/98
white garments
    Confession cleanses soul (Mary)    8/22/98
work (Labor Day)
    do fair share (Jesus)    9/7/98
world depression
    bankruptcies, spiritual (Jesus)    9/18/98
    layoffs, tax loss, turmoil (Jesus)    9/17/98
world famine
    from abused land (Jesus)    9/10/98
worrying
    accept crosses (Jesus)    7/16/98

# More Messages from God through John Leary

If you would like to take advantage of more precious words from Jesus and Mary and apply them to your lives, read the first three volumes of messages and visions given to us through John's special gift. Each book contains a full year of daily messages and visions. As Jesus and Mary said in volume IV:

*Listen to My words of warning, and you will be ready to share in the beauty of the Second Coming.* Jesus 7/4/96

*I will work miracles of conversion on those who read these books with an open mind.* Jesus 9/5/96

### *Prepare for the Great Tribulation and the Era of Peace*

**Volume I -** *July 1993 to June 1994,* ISBN# 1-882972-69-4, 256pp.          $7.95

**Volume II -** *July 1994 to June 1995,* ISBN# 1-882972-72-4, 352pp.          $8.95

**Volume III -** *July 1995 to July 10, 1996,* ISBN# 1-882972-77-5, 384pp.          $8.95

**Volume IV -** *July 11, 1996 to Sept. 30, 1996,* ISBN# 1-882972-91-0, 104pp.          $2.95

**Volume V -** *Oct. 1, 1996 to Dec. 31, 1996,* ISBN# 1-882972-97-X, 120pp.          $2.95

**Volume VI -** *Jan. 1, 1997 to Mar. 31, 1997,* ISBN# 1-57918-002-7, 112pp.          $2.95

**Volume VII -** *April 1, 1997 to June 30, 1997,* ISBN# 1-57918-010-8, 112pp.          $2.95

**Volume VIII -** *July 1, 1997 to Sept. 30, 1997,* ISBN# 1-57918-053-1, 128pp.          $3.95

**Volume IX -** *Oct. 1, 1997 to Dec. 31, 1997,* ISBN# 1-57918-066-3, 168pp.          $3.95

**Volume X -** *Jan. 1, 1998 to Mar. 31, 1998,* ISBN# 1-57918-073-6, 116pp.          $3.95

**Volume XI -** *Apr. 1, 1998 to June 30, 1998,* ISBN# 1-57918-096-5, 128pp.          $3.95